A Novel Tea

Unique ideas to enrich your life through relationships and hospitality

by Jean Chapman

Springbrook Press
Irvine, California

A Novel Tea: Unique ideas to enrich your life through relationships and hospitality

For book orders and information, you may contact the author at: www.springbrookpress.com, or in writing: Jean Chapman, P. O. Box 423, East Irvine, California 92650-0423
Phone: 949.300.6604

Cover Design by: Myriad Communication Arts
www.myriadnet.com, Huntington Beach, CA

Printed by: Ron Chapman, Kern Business Forms, Bakersfield, California

Dedicated to . . .

My Novel Tea friends and fellow-readers—Marla, Lynora, Margaret, Brenda, Lettie, Sandy, and Judy. Our times together have forged memory moments that will last me a lifetime. You have enhanced my appreciation for thought-provoking books, a pot of tea, and scintillating conversation. Thank you for your friendship and for showing up—every month!

My husband and my best friend, Larry. My deep appreciation to you for your constant support and encouragement. Over forty years of traveling together!—you've been my greatest fan in this life. Thank you for giving me the space within our marriage to *become*. You're the best!

જી

Acknowledgements

A huge "thank you" to Glenna Adamson, Judi Braddy, Lynora Weaver, Fahti Horriat, Marla Campbell, Brenda Green, and Joan Hardy. Your eagle eyes for editing detail and advice about content are greatly appreciated.

Endorsements

- *"Jean's charming book will make you want to read . . . and read. And the title alone is worth the price of the book!"* Nell Sunukjian, Director of Women's Ministries, Evangelical Free Church in Fullerton, California.

- *"I read A Novel Tea in one sitting. Throughout the reading—while enjoying a cup of tea—I thought of many ways I could take Jean's ideas and use them at my own special times with friends and neighbors."* Arlene Allen, Director of National Women's Ministries Department, General Council of the Assemblies of God.

- *"For anyone who loves to share a good read, A Novel Tea is more than just a nod and a nosh. It's a beautifully written high-tea experience with substance for the soul. Jean Chapman has given you all the tea-time tips you need to start your own Novel Tea friendship group wrapped around stories that warm, soothe and stimulate—just like a good cup of tea. Sip it slowly."* Judi Braddy, author of *Prodigal in the Parsonage; It All Comes Out in the Wash,* and *Simple Seasons: Lighthearted Lessons for Large Living.*

- *"What an incredible little book! It made me laugh and it made me cry. But more than that, it reminded me how very precious and fleeting our time on earth really is. If you long to make your life count; if you want to bring a new depth and richness to your relationships, this book is for you! Beyond sharing a cup of tea, you'll learn how to go the extra mile and discover the joy of intentional living. And along the way, you will learn to love, not just in word, but also in deed.*" Joanna Weaver, Author of *Having a Mary Heart in a Martha World: Finding Intimacy With God in the Busyness of Life,* and *With This Ring: Promises to Keep.*

- "*Jean Chapman is a gracious woman you would love to have tea with. She is a class act, well-educated, and yet can easily talk with all women. A Novel Tea is a warm, heart-felt book with many good ideas and "how-to's." It will get you excited about serving tea, reading classic literature, and developing new friends. This precious book will open your heart to smiles and tears.*" Emilie Barnes, Author and Founder of *More Hours In My Day.*

- "*Using a wonderfully broad and descriptive vocabulary, Jean paints beautiful pictures of ordinary things made special. She gives creative ideas on how to enrich your life as well as bless others—family, old friends and new acquaintances. Reading this book will be a relaxing respite. But it will also stimulate and excite you about new dimensions that are attainable for any of us."* Elnora Dresselhaus, Pastor's wife from San Diego, California.

- *"Jean has tilted the lid of her soul in this book and treated its readers to a brew of warm hearts, damp eyes, and new resolve. I have heard the rattling of the cups, and I'm on my way to the hutch. I'm determined to read from her reading list and join the tea party. This is a 'must read' that will have you mobilized. Fill up the kettle and settle in. 'One lump or two?'"* Judy Rachels, Director of Women's Ministries, Southern California District of the Assemblies of God.

- *"Ever the gifted teacher, mentor and motivator, Jean has given us a timeless treasure in A Novel Tea. Whether it is a cup of tea and a good book or some other passion of your life, this unique and inspiring book is chock-full of practical tips and creative ideas and tools for pursuing meaningful and lifelong friendships. Don't be surprised if you find yourself, as I do, picking it up to re-read from time to time!"* Glenna Adamson, wife of Arden Adamson, Superintendent of the Wisconsin-Northern Michigan District Council of the Assemblies of God.

Table of Contents

Preface

From the day we're born until the day we die, we travel through vast uncharted territories in life. I have learned some things on the journey about the human heart and connecting with other people by establishing bonds of friendship that strengthen and encourage.

"Nothing in the world is single; all things by a law divine in one another's being mingle— " wrote the poet. *A Novel Tea* is about the divine mingling of souls over a cup of tea. You will not find any instructions on how to make a pot of tea within these pages, but you will read stories that inspire you to relate to people with unique ideas and challenges to make "friends you haven't met yet!"

The farther I travel on my journey, the more aware I am of the need to be connected to people. God placed the desire and the need for communion in my soul. Those desires are acted out in my relationships with God, my family members, and my friends. But they reach outside the borders of my living, too. Obedience to cross thresholds I wouldn't ordinarily cross and give a "cup of cold water in the name of Jesus" flows out of my intimacy with God. He is teaching me that life cannot be lived merely for "self." In fact, the Holy Scriptures mandate that if we are serious about our lived-out faith, we will lay down our lives and follow the teachings of Jesus Christ.

One of the ways to do this is to be very *intentional* about what we do and how we do it. For example, I begin every day with 86,400 seconds to spend. Once a day is over, my seconds disappear into yesterday; I'll never get them back. I can waste that precious time, or I can invest it in people and reap dividends for eternity.

So how do I go about making good choices that will benefit not just me, but others whose lives I intersect on the journey?

This book tells the stories of unique opportunities and ideas to incorporate into your world; how you can adapt these ideas to meld into your particular lifestyle. In one chapter I relate how I literally present my personal planner/ calendar to God every Monday morning. As I look over my appointments and class schedule, I ask God to make me sensitive to each person I meet in the coming week. I pray for God to bless me so that I can bless others with encouragement.

What I hear everywhere I go from everyone I meet is the modern complaint: "I'm so busy! I'm on a fast track, and I can't get off." When we feel too busy, we pull into ourselves and hibernate. We retreat from people. But as followers of Jesus Christ, we can't allow ourselves to get too busy for people. Billy Graham once said, *"We hurt people by being too busy. Too busy to notice their needs. Too busy to drop that note of comfort or encouragement or assurance of love. Too busy to listen when someone needs to talk.*"

I hope and pray this book will thrust you out of some comfort zones and be a map of sorts on the path of excellence in living. Become devoted to service and by doing so, you will cultivate a fruitful life. Excellence can be achieved by taking the very simple things of life—things like a teapot, books, and a listening heart—and using them to their maximum potential.

Brew yourself a cup of tea, sit down and make yourself at home with me as you read this book. Welcome to my world! God's richest blessings on all of you who are seeking the best God has for you.

Jean Chapman, author

Please note: Although names have been changed in this book, the stories are very real.

❧ Chapter One ❧

What a Novel Idea!

"A cup of tea, fine food, and thee, my friend, with a good book wrapped up in conversation."
(Jean Chapman)

The concept of a Novel Tea evolved in a very serendipitous manner. My friend Marla and I were eating lunch at a lovely outdoor restaurant on a harbor in Newport Beach. Several weeks before, I had given her a copy of Anne Lamott's book, *Traveling Mercies*.

"Read it," I urged her, "and then we'll have lunch and discuss the book. Let me know what you think about this author's spiritual pilgrimage."

Now here we were on a balmy Southern California day, engaged in a lively conversation about Lamott and her sometimes tentative, sometimes tenacious quest in her search for God. Marla took one point of view about Lamott's journey, and I took an opposing view. The book had definitely provoked a choleric response in each of us. We took turns reading different portions of the chapters out loud to support our opinions as we probed the depths of the best-selling work. Soon we were sharing our own individual stories of discovering God at points and places in our lives.

It was one of the most mentally stimulating exchanges I had experienced in a long time. Marla, a professor at a local university, never left any doubts about her opinion. She seemed to draw an extension of life from our conversation. We finally leaned back in our chairs satiated by fine food, too many cups of tea, and the exhaustive discourse. In unison we said, "Ah, that was wonderful!"

"Wouldn't it be a novelty," I mused, "if we got together regularly with a group of women who love to read and had these kinds of discussions?"

"Yes, a novelty," Marla assented.

As though choreographed by God, we looked at each other across the table and instinctively knew what the other was thinking.

"Marla, a *Novel Tea!*" I slapped the table with excitement and beamed at my friend. "That's it! Let's start a Novel Tea."

The concept of our book club was conceived that day by two friends who had been mentally challenged by a thought-provoking, non-fiction work.

With the stimulation of our time together brewing in my mind, I jotted some ideas down on paper later that day. Who should I invite to join Marla and me in a monthly book-reading group? How should the group be organized? Obviously the size of the group would be determined by how many women could be seated around a table. They would have to be women who liked to read, and who would be comfortable engaging in conversation. I sensed God's direction as faces and names started filtering through my consciousness. I began making phone calls over the next few days. One person after another said yes, they would love to participate in a Novel Tea. A few of the women I invited were already close friends; however, there were several people I didn't know. They were friends of friends. All I knew for sure was that we liked to read and we all drank tea!

A Novel Tea was now more than an idea. I set a date and chose the book we'd read. Since I was pursuing a graduate degree in English, I conveniently—and expediently—selected a novel that I was assigned to read: Willa Cather's *Song of the Lark*. I sent out the invitations.

Our inaugural Novel Tea took place in my home. Since it was February, I used a Valentine motif for the dining room. The table was set with china and crystal, and red roses reigned at the center of the beautiful tableau. The lunch was prepared, and a teakettle sat on a back burner of the stove whistling with boiling water, ready to fill the teapot. This was the day!

One by one, old friends and new faces crossed over the threshold. Brenda, our youngest member, was the last one to arrive. She had barely walked in the door and taken off her coat when she began talking about *The Song of the Lark*.

"I'm Thea!" she cried dramatically, referring to the protagonist in Cather's novel. She was noticeably excited about the book.

"I read and cried and thought about my own background in music. This was a wonderful novel!" Her enthusiasm ignited responses in the rest of us. We chimed in with some preliminary thoughts as I lit the candles and arranged my Hawaiian chicken salad on china plates. An animated conversation had already begun, and we hadn't even sat down at the table yet. This was definitely a good sign!

As we ate and decided on whether we wanted Irish Breakfast or Earl Grey tea, Brenda elaborated on her kinship with Thea Kronborg. Like Cather's young heroine, Brenda began studying piano as a child. When she grew and went to college, she continued with her musical studies and received her B.A. in piano.

"But it was my voice that teachers eventually said I should have concentrated on," Brenda recalled wistfully. She related the parallel of her musical pursuit with that of Thea Kronborg's storyline in our novel. We listened and empathized with our friend.

We delved more deeply into different themes of the novel. We talked about the positive male role models that had influenced Thea's life and career; we discussed Cather's writing style—her insertion of Nature and the metaphors she used to correspond to the artist's experience. We sighed and smiled as we journeyed with Thea from Colorado to Chicago, to her eventual debut onto a world stage as a renowned singer. We marveled at Cather's ability to create images that let us burrow into the enclaves of a large city or hunker down into the southwestern American landscape, experiencing the vast blue sky that hung above majestic mountains chiseled into the countryside.

The time went by too quickly. The candles burned lower and lower as we savored the harmonious ambiance of friendship, delicious food, piping hot tea, and the lively discussion of a classic work. I sensed, even now in its initial stage, that a Novel Tea would evolve into a sacred time that we would come to cherish.

Before we dispersed that first lovely day, we adjourned to the living room. Brenda went to the piano and began playing the opening strains of *Caro Mio Ben,* Italian for *"Ah, Dearest Love,"* by Giordani. We thrilled to the sound of her voice singing the soulful melody. Eyes closed, she leaned over the keyboard, her blond hair falling softly around her shoulders. Her tone sometimes yearning, sometimes soaring, Brenda sang with passion and pathos.

As the final notes of the Italian Art song faded, we were reminded that a work of fiction mirrors real life. Brenda had given substance and reality to our novel with her music. We could very well have been in a concert hall in Europe as Thea made her debut into opera. Brenda imbued the character of Thea Kronborg with a heart and a soul wrapped up in flesh and blood; a woman who became a human being for us that day.

But we were in my home in Irvine, California. We were hushed in a moment that transcended time and space.

That first Novel Tea was far more than eating food or drinking tea, or even merely discussing a book. I sensed that we were beginning a monthly ritual that would prove to bind our hearts as well as our minds together in a cohesive friendship. The congruence of thinking, conversing, drinking tea and partaking of food would prove to be a sacramental ritual in our lives.

Thus in the spring of 2000, a Novel Tea was conceived and birthed, and it has made a difference in my life. Once aching with loneliness and longing for relationship with others who shared my passion for reading, I now have seven trustworthy girlfriends who show up for our book club every month.

My journal entry for that day in February describes it best: "We ate and talked and fed our souls and our intellect with gleanings from Cather's book. We fed our friendship with the rapport that is growing between us—diverse ages and backgrounds; we fed our bodies with good food and tea—my kind of day! Thank you, God, for these wonderful blessings of friendship, food, and talk and books. You bless me beyond measure!"

───────────

෨ *Reflect* ~ Is a part of my life spent in intellectual pursuit? Do I explore avenues of ideas and cultivate a thought life? Do I have friends who stimulate me mentally; who give me a different point of view about experiences and life?

૭ *Response* ~ I will find a solitary place that is quiet for a few moments each day to meditate on an idea; to read a portion of a book. I will mentally travel beyond the borders of my own world and expand my perceptions.

෨

"Just as our bodies have many parts and each part has a special function, so it is with Christ's body. We are all parts of his one body, and each of us has different work to do. And since we are all one body in Christ, we belong to each other, and each of us needs all the others" (Romans 12:4-5 NLT).

෨

"Resolve to edge in a little reading every day, if it is but a single sentence. If you gain fifteen minutes a day, it will make itself felt at the end of the year." (Horace Mann)

❧ Chapter Two ❧

You Are Precisely My Cup of Tea

"Who can tell the precise moment when friendship begins? The veil between individuals often lifts slowly, but when we see and know as we are known, we call each other 'friend.'"
(Jean Chapman)

Our Novel Tea group has eight members. We are all very different from one another, but we also have some things in common that make us compatible: our passion for reading, our faith in God, and our love for people. I think it would be a mistake to begin a reading group with women who think exactly alike—how boring! As iron sharpens iron, so we have found that our differences add dynamism and dimension to not just our discussion but also to our relationship.

Over the years, we have tacitly "agreed to disagree" on points-of-view regarding an author, themes of a novel, or how we relate themes to our personal lives. These different perceptions are what broaden our world-view and give us empathy for situations and experiences that are different from our own. We have had some intense conversations about many books, but the diverse opinions that surface are the very things that sharpen our thinking.

C. S. Lewis made some penetrating observations about friendship in *The Four Loves:* *"Friendship arises out of mere Companionship when two or more of the companions discover that they have in common some insight or interest or even taste which the others do not share and which, till that moment, each believed to be his own unique treasure (or burden). The typical expression of opening Friendship would be something like, 'What? You too? I thought I was the only one.' It is when two such persons discover one another, when, whether with immense difficulties and semi-articulate fumblings, or with what would seem to us amazing and elliptical speed, they share their vision—it is then that Friendship is born."* He continues by writing: *"Friendship must be about something."*

Reading and discussing literary classics are what our friendship is *about* in Novel Tea. What has been a unique revelation is that the kinship we feel transcends the differences in who we are in this thing of becoming friends. Perhaps it is precisely because of our differences that we bring an element of value and even intrigue to our group as a whole. Singly, standing apart, each of us is a fragment. But when we amalgamate our thinking and our personalities, we bring balance to our group and become "whole" (and yet there are those ingredients of sameness also).

Lewis goes on with his exploration of love and friendship: *"In this kind of love, 'Do you love me?' means [. . .] 'Do you care about the same truth?' [She] need not agree with us about the answer."* What a freeing thing to not have to agree about answers or points-of-view! The important thing is that we care about the same Truth. We are *"traveling companions, but on a different kind of journey. [. . .] Friends side by side; their eyes look ahead."*[1]

When I am with my reading friends, I look ahead to years of evolving into someone I am *becoming*—someone who will be influenced and sharpened by the friendship and thinking of my companions in Novel Tea.

∽

Allow me to introduce each of my book-loving friends to you. Our ages span four decades, we have different educational and career backgrounds, and our marital status is varied. As I make the presentation, imagine a tea caddy filled with an assortment of fragrant, exotic flavors. We love the blend!

Marla is a professor at Biola University. She has a doctorate in Intercultural Education. For

---

[1] Lewis, C. S. *The Inspirational Writing of C. S. Lewis: Surprised by Joy; Reflections on the Psalms; The Four Loves,* and *the Business of Heaven.* Inspirational Press. 1994. 148-49.

several years she taught English and drama at a Christian high school in northern California. She later served as a missionary in the Balkans before working as an assistant to Asia-Pacific Theological Seminary. As a credentialed minister, she brings theological and global viewpoints to our discussion. Marla has an intense personality and, with sensitivity and discernment, she integrates faith with learning in her classroom and in our monthly discussion. She's the spice in the brew of a Novel Tea. A single lady who makes intentional living her mandate, she has a passion for people, for ministry, and for God.

Margaret blends grace and wisdom and experience into our mix of personalities. Twice-widowed, she was married to stellar ministers of the gospel. Margaret was herself a minister of music and Christian education. Raised in Canada and born in more genteel times, Margaret is the most appreciative of the tea ambiance that seeps into our book club. "Girls," she teaches us gently, "this is the proper way to brew a pot of tea." And we "girls" have learned how to make a suitable brew during the years in which she has reigned over our hearts with the fragrance and gentility of her life. Margaret wrote *Dear Wiffy,* a compilation of her memoirs, several years ago. The portrait of a woman who has chosen to live a life defined by grace and dignity emerges from the pages of Margaret's book. She has bequeathed a legacy of refinement and godliness to all of us who know and love her.

Lynora is a woman of great energy and compassion who opens her heart and her home in generous hospitality. She has two grown children and is an interior designer. With her eye for detail and gift for organization, Lynora has worked for years with Women's Ministries in local churches. She also conducts monthly teas for widowed ministers' wives in Southern California. For fifteen years, this lady worked with local schools to conduct formal teas for adolescent girls and their mothers. She used the venue to educate girls about the emotional and biological issues in their transition to becoming women. Lynora brings vitality to our monthly discussions and is gifted at making personal applications of literary themes to everyday experiences.

Lettie is a remarkable woman! I have learned that when Lettie speaks, she has something of substance to say. She invariably cuts right to the heart of an author's intent or the theme of a book. After serving for over thirty years in Christian ministries around the world, Lettie experienced the heartache of divorce. God opened up wonderful career opportunities for her, however. After serving as an Assistant Superintendent for the Anaheim city school district, Lettie recently began her own business. Selling custom software that she developed for accounting procedures in school districts, Lettie travels throughout the state of California. The mother of three grown sons, she is a proud grandmother who recently remarried.

Brenda is our delightful youngest member.

As beautiful and refined as an exquisite porcelain teacup, she and her husband, Doug, pastor a church they started in the early 1990s in Brea, California. They have two daughters, Jocelyn and Charisse, and a son, Paul, who are growing up right in front of our eyes. Paul was a pre-schooler when we started Novel Tea. We all loved this solemn little guy with blonde hair and blue eyes who talked in a soft, husky voice. One day when Paul was a very little boy, he accompanied his mom to Trader Joe's. Brenda was buying goodies for a fall-themed Novel Tea. As she placed pirouette cookies and chocolate oranges in her cart, he asked her rather plaintively, "Is that stuff for your tea ladies?" (He was hoping for some goodies, too!) In another chapter I will describe a children's tea that Jocelyn and Charisse organized with Brenda's help. When Paul started kindergarten, Brenda began teaching elementary classroom music. She adores God, her family, music, and earnestly explaining why a book speaks to her.

Sandy joined Novel Tea a few years ago. I have come to appreciate Sandy's heart as I watch how willingly she helps with ministries in our church. She befriends the lonely and opens her heart and beautiful home with great generosity. Married to Joe, her high school sweetheart, and the mother of two handsome sons, Sandy experienced the wonder of becoming Madelyn Faye's grandmother in January of 2003. Enjoying the elite status of "Grandma," Sandy loves gourmet cooking, entertaining, and reading.

27

Judy is our most recent member. She has a Ph.D. in Marital and Family Therapy from Fuller Seminary and an MA in Theology and in Marriage and Family Ministry. A full-time professor at Talbot School of Theology/Biola University, Judy and her husband, Gene, have two children and six grandchildren. I asked her to describe what Novel Tea meant to her. She wrote: "We all need to be stimulated, loved, and empowered by other women who are serious about God's work in their lives, their families, their ministries, and who desire accountability. Novel Tea is like drinking a refreshing iced tea on a hot day. We go home with quieted spirits that are inspired to carry on the work of God in our lives. This happens through deep and intimate discussions of the books we have read, the vulnerability of sharing our lives together, and knowing that we are prayed for. It is truly a blessing!" Last year we were winding up a discussion about Louisa May Alcott's novel, *Little Women*. We sat around Margaret's dining room table, and Judy remarked that she had been praying to find a group of women just like all of us! What did she mean by that? She explained that she had her teaching, her church life, and family and activities, but she longed for "girlfriends" with whom she could read and discuss good books. She found us! We're blessed by her warmth. Judy has been an asset on many levels, and she has endeared herself to all of us as a friend.

Jean—I grew up in a pastor's home in an environment of hospitality, music, and reading.

My dad and mom were both avid readers. Most of Dad's books were theological in nature; however, I spied a novel on his bookshelf when I was in sixth grade—*A Lantern in Her Hand* by Bess Streeter Aldrich. (That particular book became a resource decades later for my M.A.degree in American literature.) Abbie Deal became a character with whom I lived as I smiled and cried my way through the timeless classic. My mom read every Grace Livingston Hill book ever written, and my sisters and brother and I grew up with Jo, Amy, Beth, Meg, and Laurie; Nancy Drew, the Bobbsey twins, and the Hardy boys. My childhood dream was to someday teach literature in college. But life took a detour. I married, worked to put my husband through college, eventually had children, and then worked alongside my husband in church ministry. When my husband was voted to a district officer's position for our denomination, he resigned his pastorate in Lancaster, California and we moved to Irvine, California where our church headquarters is located. With fear and trembling and a great amount of trepidation, I went back to school at the ripe old age of 48. I received my A.A., B.A., and Master's degree in English when I was over 50. I taught my first class of American literature to a group of adult students at Biola University on my 55th birthday. It was literally a childhood dream come true for me. On that educational journey, however, I was lonely for personal relationships. And then we began a Novel Tea, and the women who share books with me each month have become my friends.

So that is who we all are. We sample each delicious flavor in the tea caddy and find we love them all. Variety is the spice of life!

In today's world of stress and hectic schedules, a Novel Tea has become the porch of my life where I relax with friends. On that porch, acquaintances have become intimate friends. A myriad of books have spawned ideas and ideals that we have explored collectively. A commitment to a Novel Tea has mysteriously melded us into a cohesive sisterhood based on a passion for books, thinking out loud, and a thirst for a good cup of tea.

During these last seven years, we have been strength to each other. We have built a level of trust as we have dared to be vulnerable about some of our disappointments and heartaches. Our trust is reinforced by the confidentiality we have pledged to each other. What we share in a Novel Tea is safe with each member and stays within our borders.

In the last few years, each one of us has experienced some type of personal crises: illness, trauma with children's issues, divorce, accidents, transitions, and emotional pain. Our children have married, relatives have died. Supporting each other through the bumps, detours, highs and lows of our collective journey with phone calls, cards, meals, and a sincere love and empathy has made all the difference in the world. We are traveling together, looking forward.

If you, too, are longing for deeper friendships, you might think about getting together regularly with a group of women who share your interests. The focus of your group could be books and reading. It could be a hobby of some sort: scrap-booking, knitting, or quilting or cooking. You might seek out a fellow-straggler that is in the same season of life. Share hopes and dreams and dilemmas as you huddle together at a corner table in Starbucks to relax with a comrade. The important thing is that you simply begin to seek friendships. Think of women you don't know as "friends you haven't met yet."

William Wordsworth once wrote: *"The world is too much with us."* If the world—jobs, schedules, children, house-cleaning—is too much with you, start reading and sharing. Form a get-together that fits your personalities and schedules and lifestyles. Make an oasis in your life—a "porch"— where you can sit and explore the mysteries of friendships and thinking. You will be the richer for it. Remember, the friendships you form today will buttress you in the days ahead when the storms of life occur. You will be stronger with friends by your side.

ভ   *Reflect* ~ Who do I call my "friend"? Am I friendly to others? Do I wait behind a wall of shyness and silence for people to make the first move toward me? Are there people who would call me a friend? Do I gravitate to people who are just like me? Do I go outside of my comfort zone to cultivate friendships with people in other spheres?

ভ   *Respond* ~ I will purpose to be friendly to people. I will smile at others—even if they don't smile first or smile back! I will purpose to foster new relationships in my life periodically. Each one of us must take the initiative to show ourselves friendly if we want the world to be a friendlier place.

৩০

"Two people can accomplish more than twice as much as one [. . .] . If one person falls, the other can reach out and help. A person standing alone can be attacked and defeated, but two can stand back-to-back and conquer. Three are even better, for a triple braided cord is not easily broken."
(Ecclesiastes 4:9-12 NLT)

৩০

"To have a friend is to have one of the sweetest gifts that life can bring; to be a friend is to have a solemn and tender education of soul from day to day."
(Amy Robertson Brown)

∽ Chapter Three ∾

Organizing a Novel Tea

*"In all human affairs there are efforts, and there
are results, and the strength of the effort
is the measure of the result."*
(James Allen)

Anyone can organize a group like a Novel
Tea and format it to fit their time and personal
schedules. Our book club is rather fancy and fussy.
You may want to be far more casual when you get
together. Remember, it doesn't have to be a book
club: you can use these same guidelines to organize
any group—scrap-booking, knitting, cooking,
quilting, a home Bible study—whatever suits your
interests.

You will need to do the following things as
you plan:

📖 **Decide who to invite** to join your club and
how many members you want to include. Space
and place will determine this to a large extent. I
encourage you to consider inviting people you may
not know very well. This setting will provide an
opportunity to make new friends. I would

recommend no fewer than four women and no more than eight. Intimacy gets lost somewhere when there are too many people sharing a conversational space.

📖 **Ask each member to make a commitment** to attend for a specified period of time—three to six months will give each person an idea of whether or not this group is her cup of tea. You may also decide as a group to have some guidelines. If someone misses more than twice, you might suggest that she consider joining at a later date when it better suits her schedule. These times should be respected by everyone in your book club.

📖 **Decide on the place where you will meet.** We prefer meeting in our homes around our dining room table (or kitchen table). The ambiance is cozy and personal, and the heart of hospitality makes us feel welcome and gives a momentary separation from the world. Also, we're not distracted by servers or nearby patrons. We rotate going to each other's homes. With eight members, this means each one of us will host at least once a year. Occasionally we have gone to a local Tea Room or even a restaurant for a Novel Tea. In the next chapter, I will share ideas on how to keep all of your planning very simple. A Novel Tea is not about being complicated or difficult: it's about cultivating friends of the heart and friends of the mind. Decide on whether you want to meet in your homes—or Starbucks!

📖 **Decide on the date and the time** you will meet each month. We are very fortunate in Novel Tea that none of us has a nine-to-five job. However, several of us teach at the university level, and our schedules vary from semester to semester. We try to be sensitive and accommodating to each woman and her family's needs, her church schedule, and job requirements. At the beginning of each semester, we coordinate our calendars to see which day of the week is the most convenient. The hostess chooses the menu and whether we will have a brunch or a luncheon. We never schedule our Novel Teas during evenings or week-ends: that's family time. Now here's a strong word of advice: **Be flexible and willing to adapt** when schedules collide. Emergencies happen; unforeseen events come up at your child's school. Dates cannot be set in cement. Don't be hesitant to reschedule if it becomes necessary.

📖 **Decide who will be in charge.** Someone has to be the leader! By that I mean that there must be one person who will be the final say about your club. As equal as everyone may be and as gifted as every single member may be, someone has to be the last word on the organization of your club, handling changes that come up, and making the ultimate decisions about book selections and other meeting guidelines.

📖 **Decide on how to notify each member about dates and times for Novel Tea.** Even though you've done a master calendar, there very well may be changes that come up during the year from those initial dates. Coordinate calendars every month. Invitations (sent by the hostess) should specify the location, date, time and the title of the book you are reading. A request for an RSVP along with the telephone number of the hostess is helpful. Don't make it complicated! Very often we e-mail the group or phone each other to get the information out. But remember, that person in charge will make sure someone is doing the notifying.

Decide on the format of your meeting.
We always begin Novel Tea with our meal. We all love to cook, and we love to eat, so this works for us! Sandy is a gourmet cook, and she will often have some type of hors d'oeuvres for us to nibble on while she does last-minute meal preparation. I can't tell you how wonderful it is to cross the threshold of a friend's home each month. It is usually a month or so between the times we see each other. The feeling of "coming home" is strong as we hug each other and exchange news about our lives. Spontaneous discussion of our novel usually seeps into our conversation during the meal. When the hostess pours the tea and serves the dessert, however, we reach for our books and wander into the world of our novel. I often initiate discussion by asking some provoking questions along these lines:

- What did you think of this novel?

- Did you like it? Why or why not?
- What were some of the main themes of the book?
- What did you think of the author's style of writing?
- What were some compelling aspects of the book that moved you emotionally or spiritually?

These are the kinds of questions that open the door to discussion. You may not have to prompt any conversation at all; in fact, you may need to be highly directive in keeping everyone from talking at once. If you find that some members are quieter than others and don't enter into discussion as readily, address specific comments to them that are non-threatening: "Lynora, what was one of your favorite passages in the novel? Read a paragraph you particularly liked." She will be drawn gently into the conversation. However, trust me—if each one of you has a passion for a good book, you will never have any trouble with discussion. If anything, you will have to be careful to keep remarks focused on the works you've read and not ricochet off on tangents. Be careful that no one monopolizes the conversation.

Before it is time to leave, get your calendars and decide the time and the place for the next Novel Tea. Decide collectively what novel you will read the next month (and specify which edition if there are several), and bid each other *adieu* until the next time.

We have found that after seven years of meeting for Novel Tea, we have hit a rhythm that works for us. As I wrote earlier, the book and discussion are the matrix of our club, but the friendships are the stuff and substance of what we have become. As you begin your Novel Tea reading group, relax, be tastefully transparent when making personal applications to the book, and allow yourself to make heart connections with the other women.

📖 **Decide on the books you want to read.** We decided from the onset of Novel Tea to read classics of literature. Although we've concentrated on works of fiction from the American canon, we have ventured into British, French, and Spanish writings, also. Our novels span the ages and come from every literary time period.

There are specific reasons we chose to read classics of literature rather than Christian fiction or even religious non-fiction. All of us either teach or attend Bible study groups; we did not need another Bible study group. We desired the intellectual forays and challenges that a literary work requires. By its own definition, literature delves into the human condition in a timeless and universal fashion with profundity and depth. Our conversations have provoked a level of thinking that stretches us intellectually and emotionally.

I have included a list of books we've read at the end of this chapter. Add your own classics;

talk to librarians, teachers, or go on-line and search thousands of titles and works.

If you look at our list of books carefully, you will notice that some of them are not actually classified as "literature"—we give ourselves permission to indulge in a lighter work during busy seasons of the year. Don't hesitate to be flexible in your reading choices.

We have been together long enough now to make connections between all the different works we've read. For example, when we read John Grisham's legal thriller, *The Summons*, we made it a point to compare and contrast the very similar themes of that book with Steinbeck's classic little novella, *The Pearl*. Again, just as iron sharpens iron, it is fun to see our minds percolating, and to be able to say, "Ah, that reminds me of . . ." and the cross-referencing has begun.

Travel far, dear reader, by immersing yourself into the geography of your novel; travel the back roads of your book's historical setting. Henry David Thoreau was able to boast that "he traveled widely" even though he never left Concord, Massachusetts and the surrounding countryside. Using his imagination, he visited countries, cultures, and religions through the books he read. Fly, ride, sail around the world as you and your friends explore the vast cosmos. Allow yourself to be transported to a realm that takes you someplace far away one day each month. Let your imagination be the vehicle and your heart the navigator as you travel widely.

You've gotten some ideas now on how to begin your book club. The important thing is to take your passion for reading books, and the desire to form more intimate friendships and *just do it!* Get your calendar out, make a plan, and then carry it out. Whether you begin your reading club with comfortable old friends, or acquaintances that have the potential to become dear friends, the point is to *begin.* There will be moments of magic when hearts recognize friends by mutual insights; those moments when you utter an inner—"Aha! I like that lady!"—and the braiding of cords of friendship has begun. There are women and books out there waiting for your friendship. A book club will be the binder that networks you together.

Happy reading!

ᖌᕼ *Reflect* ~ If my calendar and my schedule partially define me—who would they say I am?

41

How would they describe me? Do I make time to think, to read, and to meditate each day? Do I have family members and/or friends who stimulate my thinking?

  Respond ~ I will start reading! The library (or Barnes & Noble, or Borders) will become a familiar place to me. I will find someone with whom I can discuss a book that I read.

∞

"'Select only strong, healthy, and good-looking young men,' he said. 'Make sure they are well versed in every branch of learning, are gifted with knowledge and good sense, and have the poise needed to serve in the royal palace. Teach these young men the language and literature of the Babylonians.' They were to be trained for a three-year period, and then some of them would be made his advisers in the royal court." (Daniel 1:4-5 NLT)

∞

"Literature is my Utopia." (Helen Keller)

∞

Following is a list of many of the books that we've read in Novel Tea over the last six years:

> *Song of the Lark*, Willa Cather
> *My Antonia*, Willa Cather

Ethan Frome, Edith Wharton
Age of Innocence, Edith Wharton
Shadows on the Rock, Willa Cather
House of the Seven Gables,
Nathaniel Hawthorne
Uncle Tom's Cabin, Harriet Beecher Stowe
Breadgivers, Anzia Yezierska
Rip Van Winkle & Legend of Sleepy Hollow,
Washington Irving
A Christmas Carol, Charles Dickens
A Tree Grows in Brooklyn, Betty Smith
A Lantern in Her Hand, Bess Streeter Aldrich
A Painted House, John Grisham
The Diary of Mattie Spenser, Sandra Dallas
Jane Eyre, Charlotte Bronte
Wuthering Heights, Emily Bronte
*The Narrative of the Captivity and Restoration of
Mrs. Mary Rowlandson*, Mary Rowlandson
Cry, the Beloved Country, Alan Paton
Cricket on the Hearth, Charles Dickens
The Poisonwood Bible, Barbara Kingsolver
The Pearl, John Steinbeck
The Fisherman's Lady, George MacDonald
The Marquis' Secret, George MacDonald
So Big, Edna Ferber
Les Miserablés, Victor Hugo
Good-bye, Mr. Chips, James Hilton
The Curtain, Agathie Christie
The Summons, John Grisham
The Christmas Box and *Timepiece*,
Richard Paul Evans
Kitchen Privileges, Mary Higgins Clark

The Hobbit, J. R. R. Tolkien
The Good Earth, Pearl Buck
Strong Poison, Dorothy Sayers
The Brothers Karamazov,
Fyodor Dostoevesky
Peace Like a River, Leif Enger
One of Ours, Willa Cather
The Looking Glass, Richard Paul Evans
A Midnight Carol, Patricia K. Davis
The Count of Monte Cristo, Alexander Dumas
Candide, Voltaire
A Tale of Two Cities, Charles Dickens
The Secret Life of Bees, Sue Monk Kidd
A Common Life, Jan Karon
Shepherds Abiding, Jan Karon
Little Women, Louisa May Alcott
Reading Lolita in Tehran, Dr. Azar Nafisi
Don Quixote, Miguel Cervantes
God's Joyful Surprise, Sue Monk Kidd
Pride and Prejudice, Jane Austen
A Light From Heaven, Jan Karon
O Pioneers!, Willa Cather
The Country of the Pointed Firs,
Sarah Orne Jewett
Sense and Sensibility, Jane Austen
The Adventures of Huckleberry Finn, Mark Twain
Alice's Adventures in Wonderland and
Through the Looking Glass
Lewis Carroll
The Great Gatsby
F. Scott Fitzgerald

ᔧ Chapter Four ᔥ

The Tea Factor: Simplicity and Serendipity

"Our life is frittered away by detail. Simplicity, simplicity, simplicity! Let your affairs be as two or three, and not a hundred or a thousand. Keep your accounts on your thumb nail."
(Henry David Thoreau)

A friend of mine is fond of saying, "The thing to remember is that the main thing *is* the main thing!" I remind myself often that drinking tea or putting on a tea or even going to a Novel Tea is only a factor of the main thing: the *main thing* is people! Connecting with people on a soul level, on a heart level, and on an intellectual level is a necessary component of my life. The point is to keep your plans simple, be alert to serendipity moments, and be intentional about the actions of your life.

Each one of us will have to analyze the details of our lives and figure out where we can simplify. Technology can be wonderful in connecting me to people, but it clutters up my daily life. When I return to my home front, often tired and needing a soothing cup of tea, I have messages to listen to and return on my telephone; I have e-mails that need to be read and responded to. There are times when my cell phone seems glued to my hand and my ear. I can't get away from noise, and I can't get away from the incessant need to respond to people—right away! I have to choose how to order those technological wonders rather than let them order me.

Simplicity

When it comes to teatime, keep it simple! Tea is merely the venue that brings people together. It is not the *thing* itself. Many young women today are far too busy to spend hours putting on a fancy tea and discussing a novel of epic proportions. In fact, some of you may hyperventilate at the thought of china and crystal and gourmet cooking. Goodness! Let me assure you that you can keep things uncomplicated and still have a very meaningful time of connecting with your friends.

Here are some ideas for you to keep the details simple:

- Work smart, keep it easy, and don't even think "fancy." My savvy niece and her girlfriends get together one morning every other week at Starbucks. They call it a "Ladies' Latté"—no children allowed. This is

mommy time. They share a baby-sitter for
their preschool kids. Because they are busy,
they keep their time to a tight one hour.
Instead of talking about a complete book,
they read one book over a period of several
weeks and evaluate just one chapter during
each latté hour. It works for them!

- If you are a working gal and desire social
  and intellectual networking, organize a book
  club that meets periodically during your
  lunch hour. You will have to keep your
  discussion of a book focused, and of course,
  the food will be incidental. The important
  thing is to read a book, be part of a dialogue,
  and connect on a heart and mind level with
  co-workers. Get together in a corner of your
  office lunchroom and travel to another world
  while you eat. You will be energized for the
  rest of the day!

- Carve out an evening in your monthly
  calendar to meet with friends. Decide if you
  want to have a meal or just coffee or tea and
  dessert. Conduct your book club in a home, a
  restaurant, or even a place like Border's or
  Barnes & Nobel. The point is to keep it
  simple. Slowly sip your tea or coffee or a
  cappuccino—whatever you like—and talk
  about that intriguing novel you've read.

- You deserve a break today! Regularly corral the kids in one of your homes, share the expense of a babysitter (or take turns staying with the wee ones), and get yourselves to McDonald's, or Wendy's, or some other fast-food place. Order your food, find a table apart from the rest of the crowd, and settle into some serious conversation and fries! It will be the break that keeps you sane, and for at least a couple of hours you will speak in complete sentences.

- Have everyone pick up their own fast food or bring a sack lunch and meet at a house. If you want to go to the trouble, empty those containers of food onto plates and use silverware, but keep it simple. If you choose to eat off Styrofoam, you can toss everything but your book after your conversation. No mess and no fuss!

Those are just a few ideas about how to keep the concept of a book club simple. It is not about the food and the table setting: it is about developing friendships, having stimulating conversation, and exploring ideas. That's the important thing—the *main* thing.

Let me share with you what Margaret did a few years ago. She wasn't quite up to cooking the day before she was scheduled to host Novel Tea, so she got on the phone and arranged an extraordinary lunch. Ringing up the posh Neiman-

Marcus Tearoom at a nearby fashion mall, she ordered popovers with strawberry butter. Then she let her fingers do the walking all the way over to the Macaroni Grill restaurant. She instructed them to prepare eight chicken Florentine salads to be ready for pick-up the next morning. She was careful to specify dressing on the side and extra parmesan cheese. For the dramatic finalé of our meal—the *piéce de résistance*—she called her friendly baker at the corner Von's supermarket and ordered tiramisu.

The following morning, I picked up all the orders for Margaret. When I arrived at her house, she had the dining room table set with her prettiest china, and the teakettle was simmering on the stove. We took food out of bags, put the popovers in a lovely basket and nestled the strawberry butter in a delicate crystal container. Tossing the salad with the dressing in a huge bowl, we arranged our main course on individual plates. Margaret put the three-layered tiramisu on a pedestal plate. The meal was gorgeous, it was delicious, and . . . she bought it! Who would have known if she hadn't told on herself?! So, you see . . . you can do this! You may not be able to afford a meal like that, but you can pick up meals at El Pollo Loco, Taco Bell, or (my favorite) Panda Express. What could be more simple?

Go and buy your food already prepared. "I can do that?" you ask. "Yes! You can do that!" Go to Trader Joe's or Sam's Club or Costco. Buy something delicious in a package—already cooked or baked—and simply camouflage it on pretty dishes with a few tricky garnishes. Presentation is everything. Unless you spill the beans, no one will know you bought your food ready-made! Even here, you can do things as simply or make them as elaborate as your budget will allow. These stores have everything from salads to main dishes to delicious desserts.

A couple of years ago, I made Swedish meatballs for a Christmas Novel Tea luncheon. I bought the meatballs at Sam's Club. Counting out the number of meatballs I needed (I put the rest back in the freezer for later use), I browned them in a little oil in my skillet. Using a slotted spoon, I put them aside on a plate while I made a roux from some butter and flour mixed with the bits of meat in the pan. I slowly stirred in canned chicken broth. When the gravy was nicely thickened, I blended in sour cream and put the meatballs back in the pan before I added the final ingredient— lingonberry jam. Spooned over a bed of rice and served with a bright green salad, it was such an easy luncheon. A word of caution, however, is that even though this is an easy dish to make, it does still take some time.

Whether you cook, get take-out food, or buy it from Sam's Club, keep your preparations as simple as you need them to be. Remember, the main thing is that you want people to experience the hospitality of your heart that says, "Welcome to my home. Come to the table." It's not about entertaining or impressing women; it's about acceptance. Nothing does that like breaking bread together around a table.

Serendipity

There are magical moments of serendipity that occur when you least expect them—unplanned, unscheduled moments that bless you and fill you with wonder. Be on the lookout for them and even set the stage for them to occur. These moments, too, can be the main thing, but you may not know it until you're looking back at the memory and saying, "That was wonderful!"

Let me share some memories of serendipity intervals in my life. My daughter loves to get alone with a book or her journal and a cup of tea. She's a thinker. When she went back to college to finish her degree, she came home to live with us for several years. It was an adjustment for her to live with Mom and Dad again after being on her own. It was also an adjustment for us to have offspring returning to our nest. However, love and grace made the transition possible.

Annie's schedule was hectic with classes, studying, and a part-time job. Our lives were busy with speaking, jobs, and studying (I was in school getting my degree in English). There were those moments, however, when Annie would call down from her upstairs study, "Have you got a few minutes, Mom?"

Of course I had a few minutes! No matter what I was involved with, I laid it aside and put the teakettle on. When my daughter wanted a few moments of my time, I had learned to drop everything. "Just a minute," or, "I don't have time right now," meant a lost opportunity to link hearts with my girl.

I have precious memories of those last couple of years that Annie lived with us. When she made those requests for my presence, I put the water on to boil. Putting tea things on a pretty tray that was always within reach, I prepared Annie's favorite tea. As I crossed the threshold of her room with my offering, her delighted face was all the reward I needed. She wanted my presence and listening ear; I entered her *place* with a tray of tea and a listening heart. Those moments became sacred rituals that were meaningful building blocks between me and my daughter. Those are moments that are indelibly written on the slate on my memories. I don't even remember things we talked about, but I do remember how I felt watching her face as we talked, both curled up on the couch, sipping tea. It was an unhurried, serendipity moment in an otherwise frenetic day.

Brenda arranged a serendipity outing for us several years ago in the merry month of May. Her husband, Doug, had their house turned inside-out with a remodeling project. Instead of despairing over her hosting assignment, Brenda made reservations at the Springfield Teahouse in downtown Fullerton. When we walked across the spacious porch to the front door of the restored white house, we were made welcome by a smiling, gracious hostess. Bowing her head slightly, she motioned to a nearby hat tree and asked us to choose a feather boa and a *chapeau* from their colorful selection. We were like little girls, giggling and twirling our boas as we preened and postured in front of mirrors in the entryway. What fun! The boas tickled our fancy, and the romantic hats harked back to an era of Victorian charm.

Seated at a lovely table overlooking Main Street, we nibbled on egg salad and cucumber tea sandwiches and discussed *So Big* by Edna Ferber. Our heroine wore an old farmer's hat, and we grubbed down in the soil of our story along with Selina Dejong as the flowers and feathers on our hats bobbed up and down in furious sympathy.

This very serendipitous novel tea became one of our more memorable occasions. We learned that being flexible and adaptable presented us with an unexpected time of fun and delight.

Plan serendipity times of discovery—go on a field trip. Often a book will have geographical or historical markers. If you live close to a location mentioned in your novel, take a visit to that place as a group. In another chapter, I relate a visit we made to a cemetery. An Angel of Hope was the centerpiece of the book by Richard Paul Evans that we were reading that month. Visiting the actual statue made our book come alive for us.

If your book mentions a painting that is perhaps on display at a local museum, by all means go visit the museum. Take your books with you. Sit in front of the painting and read portions of the book aloud to each other. In one of our first Novel Teas, we read Cather's, *Shadows on the Rock.* Since the setting is Quebec, Canada, Margaret spoke with nostalgia and enthusiasm about the winters of that city—the ice-skating and the brittle cold. Lynora brought framed watercolor prints she had of Quebec, the city set high on a hill. Their visual and verbal details connected the geographical details of the book with the lives of our characters.

To be open to moments of serendipity, one must be *attentive*—tuned in to what is happening at the present moment, and what potential may be packed into the possibility of the moment. To be attentive is to be aware, and to be aware is to suck all the juices out of life. The main thing is to come to the end of a day, the end of a life and say, "The serendipity moments have made all the difference."

Tea is only a factor of relationships. The main thing is to keep things simple (don't let the details overwhelm you), and be open to those unplanned, unexpected opportunities of serendipity. Remember: the main thing is the *main thing!*

༄ *Reflect* ~ How could I make my life more simple? Do I do too much? Are my plans too elaborate? Do I allow divine interruptions that become building-blocks of blessing in my life?

༄ *Respond* ~ I will be creative and simplify my life in those areas that are too complicated. I will not try to do more things than I am humanly capable of doing. I will be attentive to the moments of my day and aware of the possibilities each moment presents.

ഗ

"Look here, you people who say, 'Today or tomorrow we are going to a certain town and will stay there a year. We will do business there and make a profit.' How do you know what will happen tomorrow? For your life is like the morning fog—it's here a little while, then it's gone. What you ought to say is, 'If the Lord wants us to, we will live and do this or that.' Otherwise you will be boasting about your own plans, and all such boasting is evil." (James 4:13-16 NLT)

"I've stopped thinking all the time of what happened yesterday. And stopped asking myself what's going to happen tomorrow. What's happening today, this minute, that's what I care about. I say: what are you doing at this moment, Zorba? . . . I'm kissing a woman. Well, kiss her well, Zorba! And forget all the rest while you're doing it; there's nothing else on earth, only you and her!" (Zorba, in *Zorba the Greek*, by Nikos Kazantzakis)

✤ Chapter Five ✤

The Path of Intentional Relationships

*"In shining old shoes or old silver, it don't make no
difference what brand of polish you uses. You has got to
mix elbow grease with it to make it shine."*
(Early American Folk Wisdom)

Have you heard the saying, "The road to hell
is paved with good intentions?" There are several
variations of that quotation, but basically it means
that if a good intention doesn't end in a concrete
action, it is meaningless. How can we cross the
great divide of intentions and charge through the
portals of making things happen?

The path to making our good intentions come
to pass is paved with three D's: Determination,
Discipline, and Diligence.

Intentions begin as thoughts in our minds
and feelings in our hearts. We must determine
that if we think about something and have a desire,
then we must *do* something to make it happen.
Determination is a stepping stone. If I have the
intention of inviting someone to my house for
dinner, I need to pick up the phone at the first
opportunity, give an actual invitation, and then put

the date on my calendar. It sounds so simple, but to carry through on our thoughts and to make them happen require conscious action.

There is an amount of *self*-discipline required to carry out good intentions. Habits become disciplines; disciplines become habits. I have to exercise a control of the *self* and make myself do what I should do. It helps to focus on the long-term rewards of carrying out an intention. Instant gratification can kill the determination and discipline necessary to stay aware of the end goal or result of my intentions.

Diligence means simply staying consistent in my efforts to carry through with my intentions—staying the course. If I am willing to work hard and remain intent on the goal that is set before me, I will be well on my way to accomplishment and achievement.

Henry David Thoreau, one of our great American authors, determined at one point in his life to live intentionally. He was tired of mediocrity and uniformity. He left the organized life of Concord, Massachusetts to live on the edge of Walden Pond for a period of time. In the book that resulted from the time of introspection and observation, he wrote his purpose in retreat: *"I went to the woods because I wished to live deliberately, to front only the essential facts of life, and see if I could not learn what it had to teach, and not when I came to die, discover that I had not lived. I did not wish to live what was not life, living is so dear.*"[2]

Like Thoreau, I want to live intentionally; however, I have to do it right here in my own house, with my family, in the middle of a city. If I use determination, discipline, and diligence in carrying out my intentions, I will have meaningful relationships in my life, and I will feel a sense of purpose when I get up each morning.

I am learning to give God my calendar on Monday mornings. "Okay, look at my week with me, Lord. You see my schedule and who I will be meeting with. What can *we* do to make my time with them meaningful? What can I say, what can I do to encourage their hearts?" I am learning, too, that if a face starts filtering through my consciousness, if a little voice seems to whisper somewhere in my soul, "You need to call so-and-so," then I *have* to respond to those inner urges. That is God nudging me. Responding to those thoughts means that I am crossing a very fragile line between mediocre relationships and excellence in how I pay attention to people and life.

How can I give my-*self* to that someone? You may want to do what a friend of mine has done. She is a pastor's wife who moved with her family to a new neighborhood. As a way to get to know her neighbors better—and because she says she is basically shy—she started a "Neighbor's Reading Club." She wanted to establish some common ground that would hopefully evolve into

---

[2] Thoreau, Henry David. *Walden.* Everyman Publisher. 1910. 72.

friendships based on a love of books. I love that concept! Anyone can make new friends *and* start a book club or any other kind of club depending on like interests. The important thing is that you are connecting with people. Look around your neighborhood, your office, your church and ask God for some intentions that you can carry out and in the process, make some friends and be a friend.

Ask yourself these questions as you contemplate your days and the people who cross your path:

- Who do I need to be aware of? My neighbor? A co-worker? A family member? The homeless woman on the corner?
- How can I give my-*self* to that someone? Maybe all I need to do is smile as I look into her eyes; say a prayer for him or her. Can I spare five dollars for the one who is hungry?
- Do I listen attentively to people? Do I hear with my heart and my mind?
- Is there someone I can encourage by sending a card or a note?
- Is there someone I should call on the phone? Send a quick e-mail?
- How can I enhance a moment when someone drops by my house? A cup of tea? A cup of coffee?

Remember, it's not so often what we say to others as the mere fact that we are *listening* to them—we are *hearing* their hearts. In a world where people hibernate away from others, it is important to make ourselves available when others need the connection of a caring human being— whether they know it or not. You will edify someone in ways you will perhaps never know this side of eternity.

Intentional living makes all the difference in your quality of life; it makes all the difference in the world to your friends and family. I am asking God to sear *Attentiveness* and *Intentionality* into my soul. If I allow Him to do that, it will mark me as His, and it will mark my life as having been fully lived when I come to the end of my time on earth. Life is a series of moments that become sacred when we pay attention to them.

❧ *Reflect* ~ Do I look at my calendar each week with an eye for the opportunities to touch the heart of others? Do I live deliberately, or am I caught up in non-thinking moments of momentum that are meaningless? Who needs my love and attention?

❧ *Respond* ~ I will look at my calendar and commit my days to God's sensitive direction. I will purpose to act out my good intentions through determination, discipline, and diligence.

෨

"Trust in the LORD with all your heart; do not depend on your own understanding. See his will in all you do, and he will direct your paths. Don't be impressed with your own wisdom. Instead, fear the LORD and turn your back on evil. Then you will gain renewed health and vitality." (Proverbs 3:5-7 NLT)

ဆ

"... two main components of a life of optimal happiness and meaningful purpose include loving relationships and meaningful work."
(G. Ken Goodrick)

‰ Chapter Six ‱

Mentoring for Life

"A stone thrown into a pond creates waves which are practically imperceptible before they reach the shore. A shout thrown into the air re-echoes for a few moments, then dies away forever. But the life of Jesus, sacrificially thrown into the lives of His disciples, kindled there a new life that has never died away."
(Walter Marshall Horton)

Life is a journey. An American poet wrote, "I tramp a perpetual journey." Physically, emotionally, spiritually, relationally, intellectually, and through different seasons of life, we all tramp a journey that is constant and sometimes difficult and frustrating. We need help along the way. It is as difficult as threading a needle in the shadows as it is to stumble along without a mentor or a teacher—a guide who has already walked a few miles ahead of us on the path. We need someone who will encourage us to be steady and to persevere along trails that sometimes veer off into an uncharted maze. That someone is a mentor.

Sometimes we choose a mentor with great care and consideration. More often than not, however, we simply observe people and are influenced by their example.

My definition of a mentor is that she is a model: someone who comes alongside and instructs and influences a younger person by passing on truths and precepts that she has learned in the schoolroom of life. Mentoring is a "hands-on" learning laboratory for those who desire instruction from someone who has gained maturity and stability—and one who is still learning herself. In other words, a mentor is usually someone who can say, "Been there! Done that! Follow me."

Who should be a mentor? Who should seek a mentor? Everyone! Young people, single people, married people; those who are in need of spiritual or career advice need a mentor. People from every single strata of society need the help of a trusted guide. Mentors don't need to have a professional job description or title, however. They are simply people who evidence common sense, and who have learned some things over their lifetime—often through their own mistakes.

My mother was and still is a mentor to me— not by what she taught me with her words so much, but by what she modeled with her living. She loves God with all of her heart, and her life has been exemplary in *showing* what it means to be a practicing Christian. When I have had questions about how to be a wife, a mother, or how to handle personal crises, I look back at the pattern of my mom's experience. She evidenced steadiness throughout the many tribulations on her journey.

She is the first to ruefully admit, "I am not perfect! I have made so many mistakes." But she has never wavered from her commitment and loyalty to God and her family, she is full of common sense, and she is a virtuous woman.

My darling daughter, Annie, has guided me on my inner journey. Showing me and sometimes gently reminding me, she has encouraged me to take care of my soul—to guard my heart. She has directed me to books that have given me much-needed wisdom about developing healthy boundaries in my life.

My husband constantly teaches me by example as we sometimes plod, sometimes dance down the road together. Over the forty years of our marriage, he has taught me about perseverance and "hanging tough." My melancholy personality has often been in dire need of his steadfastness. When experiences and emotions have threatened to sweep me away into some nebulous maelstrom, he has held onto me tightly and kept my feet on the ground.

In American society today, women perhaps need mature, wise voices of a mentor more than any other group of people. We struggle with self-identity. We have labels plastered all over our roles: "stay-at-home moms," "working mother," "single women," "single mom"—the list goes on and on. The bottom line is that women need women! An older, experienced woman who teaches and models the "how to's" of life can assist younger women.

The Bible instructs older women to teach the younger women by example: *"Guide older women into lives of reverence [. . .] models of goodness. By looking at them, the younger women will know how to love their husbands and children, be virtuous and pure, keep a good house, be good wives. We don't want anyone looking down on God's Message because of their behavior"* (Titus 2:3-5 *The Message*). It is provocative that in our sexually-saturated society, women need to be taught *how* to love their husbands and children. Older women must teach younger women by their example and by their gentle admonition.

Women today need to be encouraged and edified. They're often overwhelmed with the duties of motherhood and demands on their time. Sometimes they have husbands who are not sensitive to their needs. Many women are single mothers who desperately need connection with not just other women, but a connection with whole, nuclear families that will show their children the roles a mother *and* a father play in a family's life.

In the nineteenth century, Sarah Moore Grimké wrote about the pivotal role of women in the home and in society: *"Let no one think [. . .] that I regard a knowledge of housewifery as beneath the acquisition of women. Far from it: I believe that a complete knowledge of household affairs is an indispensable requisite in a woman's education,— that by the mistress of a family, whether married or single, doing her duty thoroughly and understandingly, the happiness of the family is increased to an incalculable degree, as well as a vast amount of time and money saved."* She acknowledged that women should be educated beyond the culinary and manual operations of a home because, *"The influence of women over the minds and character of children of both sexes, is allowed to be far greater than that of men. This being the case by the very ordering of nature, women should be prepared by education for the* performance of *their sacred duties as mothers and as sisters [. . .] ."*[3]

It is important to teach mothers by word and example that they are performing a sacred duty in "training up a child in the way he or she should go" (Proverbs 22:6 NAS). We will do much to reinforce to them that the role they play in raising their children is vitally important and of great value to not just themselves, but to all of society. The godly mother is fitting her children to be virtuous, responsible citizens of the next generation. It is essential that on every level a woman who is a stay-at-home mom feels a sense of worth in the role she plays. That value certainly must come from the Christian community, but also from all of us who know what she is feeling and what she is experiencing as she teaches and trains her children.

I learned from personal experience just how necessary it was to pay attention to the struggles of

---

[3] Grimké, Sarah Moore. from *Letters on the Equality of the Sexes, and the Condition of Women,* "Letter VIII, The Condition of Women in the United States."

young women who were marginalized by their schedules and their role as "mother."

There was a time when I saw the need in our church for older women to mentor younger women based on the Titus pattern. How did we know that? The younger wives and mommies pleaded for some quality time with us. They weren't just asking for help; they were begging us for relationship.

The pastoral staff wives and the Women's Ministry board read books and researched mentoring programs. We sought the advice of other church groups that had mentoring programs in place. We interviewed young women about the needs in their lives. We were all struck with one thing in particular: every single young woman that came to us needed encouragement. She didn't have any sense of value in her role as a mother. "I feel so guilty that I'm *just* a housewife," "that I'm *just* a stay-at-home mom," they told us tearfully.

We knew that society certainly wasn't going to reinforce her value. It was up to us to support these women. We spent weeks organizing a mentoring program. We solicited the aid of godly older women who were diligent in teaching God's Word, who took delight in praying with women, and who were quick to display hospitality. The countenance of their faces said, "I'm approachable. I can be trusted. I will love you and accept you." We enlisted their help.

We paired an older woman with one or two younger women who would meet on a regular basis. Over a period of time, women signed lists to be protégées in our program. We held a lovely, formal Titus Tea in our hospitality center at church in order to bring the two generations of women together.

The room was lovely with round tables covered with linens, set with fine china, and vases filled with fragrant, full-blown roses. We described the "Heart-to-Heart" program. We explained the guidelines of the relationships: the length of each mentoring session, how often they would meet, and where the meetings would take place (some wanted to meet in their homes; others at the mall, or a restaurant or Starbucks). We explained the need to honor the time-frame for these sessions—the necessity to be prompt and not to over-stay the designated time. Many young women felt a blush of hope in their hearts that day as we sipped tea and made new acquaintances.

I selected four gals from the list of protégées. I already knew them. Each one was in a Bible class I taught at church. Individually, they had come to me at some point and shyly wondered if I could ever spend some one-on-one time with them.

At first I met with each woman by herself. One afternoon every other week, I brewed a pot of tea and invited my "girl" to come to my home and sit at my table. I soon discovered that it was unrealistic to meet that often with four women separately. Within two months, I joined them into one group. I knew instinctively that they would be compatible with each other. They were about the same age, they each had an area of hurt in their growing-up lives, and they had sons about the same age. A couple of the gals who were very quiet and not given to much talking became more transparent as they heard the other two converse about their lives. "You've experienced that, too?" they exclaimed after several sessions together. They were sure they were the only ones who had ever struggled with parent, husband, or child-raising issues. The shared experience of "What? You too?" became a great source of strength and comfort as they linked hearts with fellow-travelers.

I have fond memories of the four women I mentored and our times together. At first they were my assignment. Our association was one of an older woman lending maturity and experience to four younger wives and moms. Our conversations usually began with questions such as: "How do you . . . ?" or, "What do you do about . . . ?" But over time there was a subtle shift in our relationship to a middle ground that consisted of mutual respect and friendship. A special, personal bond was fashioned between the five of us during those two years of sitting around my table and partaking of tea every other week.

These women changed right before my eyes. They gained a confidence in themselves. I pointed them to the sovereignty of God over and in their lives. We prayed together for all of our needs. We became friends. Even though I was the mentor, I was vulnerable with them about the mistakes I'd made as a parent. I urged them to be aware of the season they were in with their children. I encouraged them not to stay stuck in the rut of hurt from their childhoods; to move on with their lives.

I was careful to point each of my younger friends to God's Word. Tears trickled down their cheeks as they spoke of hurts from childhood. We put our offerings of pain on the table. We looked back on our lives and faced the hurts that had scarred us, the people who had wounded us. I urged each one to turn her head and her heart and to live her life forward—moving on into the healing and richness that Jesus Christ had for her. We all had a tendency to get locked in the labyrinth of looking backward. We prayed together and spurred each other on to a "forward-looking" future. We read the words of the apostle Paul and were inspired: *"I am still not all I should be, but I am focusing all my energies on this one thing: forgetting the past and looking forward to what lies ahead, I strain to reach the end of the race and receive the prize for which God, through Christ Jesus is calling us up to heaven"* (Philippians 3:13-14 NLT).

After eight years of serving as pastors of that wonderful church in the Mojave Desert, my husband was elected by the ministers in our Southern California district to an executive office. Larry had to resign as the pastor, and we moved to Irvine, California where our district church headquarters is located. It was very painful to leave my areas of ministry with people I loved and in whom I had invested time. I was going to miss being the pastor's wife terribly!

The women I had mentored now prayed for me and put their arms around me at a particularly difficult juncture of my life. They were the ones who now pointed me to a forward-looking future even as they wept with me.

I wondered how my friends would do without me. I instructed them to be very intentional about nurturing their friendship after I was gone. "Become best friends. Get together often for tea. Pray with each other. Invite each other over to your homes for family dinners. Make sure your sons become friends. Provide a setting in which your husbands can get to know each other." The instructions went on and on. They smiled patiently at their "Mama Jean" and promised to do everything I suggested.

My girls gave me a farewell tea at Mary's house before I left Lancaster and moved to Irvine. We sat around the table, Mary and Linda and Janne and Chris and I, and reminisced about the sovereign orchestrating God had done in bringing the five of us together. We made a covenant to continue our friendship across the miles.

Before I departed that day, my girls presented me with an exquisite pink porcelain tea set inlaid with deep-pink roses. The moment was poignant. I had journeyed far with my friends. We had looked backward and moved forward. We had partaken of tea at my table for two years, and now we were partaking of a sacramental last tea. We had begun the journey as a mentor and students; now we were friends.

Today my pink tea set rests in a hallowed spot in my hutch—almost too beautiful to use. But when I touch the teapot, I'm touching the faces of my girls. I am reminded of them, and I pray for them. I can never forget them.

(As of this writing, thirteen years after that farewell tea, these women still call each other *friend*. We meet every January for an annual tea and celebrate the friendship that was divinely inspired. We are *forever* friends!)

Mentoring and spiritual guidance are organized programs and ministries in many churches and other arenas. Often a mysterious alliance of two women—usually one who is older and one who is younger—is forged as the finger of God nudges them together. They tramp the perpetual journey side by side, one leaning perhaps more heavily on the shoulder of the other, but they are moving forward. They come together initially in a learning relationship, but time connects them in bonds of love.

Allow your life to be overlapped by another's experience. You will discover that mentoring will bestow *life*, and for the rest of your life, you will benefit from the mentoring relationship.

The Middle-Age Stage

Not every mentoring relationship involves an older woman-younger woman. I have found that in today's society, many women in their forties and fifties need a guide through the middle-age stage.

Sometimes they need a push! They are wondering if their life is over now that the kids are grown and their nest is empty. I have encouraged many women with the story of my own entrance into the academic world later in life. I obtained a coveted college degree when I was over fifty. When they stand in front of me, discouraged, feeling like the definition of "mother" no longer fits, I look at them and tell them emphatically, "You have a marvelous life ahead of you! Life is an adventure!" I ask them, "What were your dreams and passions when you were younger? What imaginative games did you play when you were a child?"

I inspire many with the details of Gail Sheehy's current research on the prospects of middle-aged women: If a woman has been cancer-free and heart-disease free, she is in the infancy of her second adulthood. Because of medical technology, she has the last third, maybe even the last half of her life to live as she chooses, to pursue a new career; to dream big dreams, to chase after rainbows. She can be as creative and productive in the later stage of her life as she desires.

Sheehy's research details that by the time a woman is in her mid-forties, she knows who she is. She doesn't struggle with self-identity issues as much as she may have earlier in life.[4] That is good news for women! If you are struggling with the transition of middle age, seek out someone who has successfully traversed the bridge of middle-age.

---

[4] Sheehy, Gail. *New Passages: Mapping Your Life Across Time.* Random House: New York. 1995.

Form a relationship with her, ask her questions and listen to her advice. I must caution the reader, however, that there is hard work involved. We tend not to value things that come to us easily.

If you want to change direction in your life, set a goal, work diligently, seek encouragement from an older, trusted guide and hang in there! She will be a last-half-of-your-life director encouraging you to keep tramping as you pursue dreams later in life.

∽

Take a step back from your life for a moment and examine it carefully. Sometimes we think the journey is the *thing;* the journey gets our focus and energy as we keep plodding along toward a hazy finish line. I have learned through the seasons of my life that *the journey itself is the destination.* What do I mean by that? Let me tell you a story.

Years ago, when I was in the sixth grade, my mom and dad decided to take a driving vacation. They packed our '56 Ford sedan with suitcases and five kids and headed to Florida. We lived in Wisconsin. Imagine taking a journey with five kids who ask the incessant questions, "Are we there yet? When are we going to get there?" That trip was interminable—or so it seemed at the time.

Along the way, though, we drove through Chicago, Indianapolis, and Louisville, Kentucky and through the Blue Ridge Mountains of Tennessee. The vistas were beautiful. We stopped to see the sights that I'd only read about in books.

Winding up roads with hair-pin turns, we made our way to the top of Lookout Mountain. In the place that history has stamped as the "Battle Above the Clouds," we imagined the great Civil War battle that had been fought on that piece of land in 1863.

Before we reached our destination of Sarasota, Florida, we went through the Florida Everglades. The vast swampland was mysterious with lacy cypress trees dripping with Spanish moss. We held our breath as we peeked out from behind Dad trying to catch a glimpse of an alligator or crocodile. This landscape was very different from the pastoral richness of Wisconsin. I was overwhelmed with the wonders of nature.

The trip itself only took a few days, but I smile now as I remember back. All we children could think of during the journey was, "When are we going to get there?" Now I remember the wonders of the trip that were stops along the way. They were as much a part of the journey as the destination of my mom's cousin's house in Sarasota, Florida.

The travels of my life have been filled with different roles, varied seasons, and assorted geographical areas of the country that I have called home. But each place has been a destination on the journey. I am a daughter and a wife, a mother and a sister on that journey. I was a student on that journey, and now I am a teacher and a writer. I have worked full-time, raised children, and now have lovely days to myself that I script. The journey, every facet of it, has been the destination.

The ultimate spiritual guide for me is God and His Word. I have counseled many women, and some of the advice and insight I give them comes from my own experience. I would err greatly, however, if I did not point each one ultimately to the greatest spiritual guide that is available: God himself who works in our minds and hearts through the Holy Spirit. Scripture reveals that He—the Holy Spirit—will be our teacher and lead us into all truth.

I often go to the promises of God's Word when I'm confused about the future: *"Trust in the LORD with all your heart; do not depend on your own understanding. Seek his will in all you do, and he will direct your paths"* (Proverbs 3:5-6 NLT). It is not always easy to "trust in God with all of my heart," but it is something I am learning to do. Each time I have given him the unknowns and the imponderables of my life, God has given me direction. Now, at this point in my journey, I know God has guided me and directed me at every stage of my journey. His *"Word is a lamp to my feet, and a light to my path"* (Psalm 119:105 NLT).

In Jeremiah, God assures His people: *"'I know the plans I have for you. They are plans for good and not for disaster, to give you a future and a hope. In those days when you pray, I will listen. If you look for me in earnest, you will find me when you seek me. I will be found by you,' says the LORD. 'I will end your captivity and restore your fortunes. I will gather you out of the nations where I sent you and bring you home again to your own land*'" (29:11-14 NLT). I love those verses! God knows my past—the spiritual and emotional captivity I've been in—the "backward" reality of my history. But He has plans that are good for me. He has a future and a hope for me! God promises that—how wonderful!

Where are you on the journey? Remember, where you are now is not where you will be in five years or ten years. Keep your bags packed and always be ready for the next leg of the trip.

∾ *Reflect* ~ Do I examine my life and my living? Do I need to seek advice and counsel from a wiser, older woman about the vagaries of my life? Do I turn to God for Truth and spiritual wisdom?

∾ *Respond* ~ I will spend quiet time in contemplation; I will examine every area of my life. I will seek out the wisdom and maturity of an older woman that I respect. I will look at my past and understand it and come to grips with it, but then I vow to live the rest of my life forward!

ଚଚ

"My child, listen to me and do as I say, and you will have a long, good life. I will teach you wisdom's ways and lead you in straight paths. If you live a life guided by wisdom, you won't limp or stumble as you run. Carry out my instructions; don't forsake

them. Guard them, for they will lead you to a fulfilled life." (Proverbs 4:10-13 NLT)

ം

"I am a little pencil in the hand of a writing God who is sending a love letter to the world." (Mother Teresa)

~~ Chapter Seven ~~

Tea and Empathy

"A friend is one to whom one may pour out all
the contents of one's heart, chaff and grain together,
knowing that the gentlest of hands will take
and sift it, keep what is worth keeping, and with
a breath of kindness blow the rest away."
(author unknown).

Marla and I have been friends now for many
years. In the beginning of our relationship, and
true to Aristotle's astute observation that the wish
for friendship develops rapidly but friendship does
not, we took an immediate liking to the other when
we met, but the friendship came more slowly. Love
and friendship in their highest form need time and
intimacy to develop. One cannot hurry friendship
along or force the *knowing* that is required. The
actual intimacy of close friendship is forged over
time and eventually develops into trust and
acceptance. The *process* of becoming friends took
awhile.

An old proverb says that "you cannot get to
know each other until you have eaten the

proverbial quantity of salt together." How can one person truly become intimate with another unless she eventually, little by little, risks baring her heart with all of its layers of imperfection *and* virtue? Somehow the transparency and vulnerability lowers the veil between friends and we accept the other, not because she is perfect, but because she is human.

The preliminary phase of our friendship began when Marla moved to Orange County in Southern California to finish her doctoral dissertation at Talbot School of Theology/Biola University. To Marla, home was still Fremont in northern California. One day Marla took a break from her writing and called me on the telephone. She was frustrated with the hibernation necessary for her writing. She lamented the feelings of dislocation and disorientation with which she was wrestling.

I could relate fully with my new friend. Seven years earlier we had moved to Orange County from our pastorate in Lancaster, California. I missed the landscape and skies of the immense Mojave Desert, our church family, and the ministries in which I had been involved. For a long time I felt like I had lost my bearings. I wondered who I was supposed to be now that I was no longer a pastor's wife. And my nest was empty with both of my kids in college. I truly thought my life was over until I went back to school to begin my studies in literature. So when Marla verbalized her feelings of isolation and not belonging anywhere, I knew exactly what she was talking about.

But I didn't give Marla sympathy: I gave her empathy. Pity is not necessarily a positive emotion. When we pity someone, we feel sorry for them. We may shed a few tears for their plight or misfortune; we might tell them, "I'm so sorry," and mean it. But at the end of the day, unless we have experienced what someone else has experienced, we cannot hunker down into the trenches of their heartache with them.

Warren Wiersbe writes that, *"[. . .] we are loving channels of the grace of God."* He quotes an eleventh-century monastic: *"Justice seeks out the merits of the case, but pity only regards the need."*[5] Pity sheds true tears of compassion but often fails to share the yoke of sorrow.

Empathy, on the other hand, is defined as "the projection of one's own personality into the personality of another in order to understand the person better; ability to share in another's emotions, thoughts, or feelings." This is exactly what the sacred scriptures admonish us to do as we feel a person's misfortune: *"Share each other's troubles and problems, and in this way obey the law of Christ"* (Galatians 6:2 NLT). Because I cared about Marla and because I had once stumbled along the same path that she was now traveling, I could identify with her feelings of being uprooted and lost.

---

[5] Wiersbe, Warren. *On Being a Servant of God.* Nashville: Thomas Nelson, Publisher. 1993. 14.

Marla needed the distraction of some fun times! I formulated a plan to have some girlfriend outings and start creating some memories for Marla in her new geographical home. My plan was birthed out of empathy. Marla loves the ocean and Andrea Bocelli and conversation and good food and reading. I coordinated a day that we blocked out on our calendars—a whole day away from our graduate studies. We headed for the coast. Brunching in Newport Beach, we talked and laughed for a couple of hours over a relaxing lunch and a view of the bay. It was out of this time together, by the way, that a Novel Tea was conceived. This was the day we discussed LaMott's book, *Traveling Mercies*, and examined that author's spiritual journey.

When I wasn't looking, Marla had popped the CD of her favorite Italian singer, Andrea Bocelli, into the CD player of my car and turned up the volume button. When we got in the car to leave, I turned the key in the ignition and almost jumped through the roof at the sudden explosion of sound. The famous Italian was bellowing out an opera tune from my car's stereo system. Marla loves to have a good time and roared with laughter at my surprise. We rolled the windows down, let the wind blow through our hair, and turned the volume even higher as we headed south on Pacific Coast Highway.

We ended up at a coffee house somewhere in lovely Laguna Beach and sipped lattés late in the afternoon as an orange sun hung suspended on the horizon of the ocean. The respite seemed to give Marla a new lease on living—for that day, anyway—and the break from our schedules was good for both of us.

A couple of weeks later, Marla walked in the back door of my kitchen. I had known she would be dropping by, so I had the teakettle on. Not really paying too much attention to Marla or the tea for that matter, I was gripped in one of those rushing-around kinds of mornings. I pulled out barstools from under my kitchen counter and grabbed mugs from my cupboard. We chatted as I poured the tea and continued to busy myself in the kitchen. I stood at the kitchen sink with my back to Marla, washing up some dishes. And then I stopped. There was something in the tone of her voice. I turned around and looked at my friend . . . really looked at her this time. Tears glimmered in her eyes.

"What's wrong?" I asked.

Marla's face collapsed in despair. Perching on the edge of her barstool and dabbing furiously at her eyes with a Kleenex, she sobbed out a litany of woe: her dissertation deadline was nagging her day and night, she was anxious to find a place of her own to live; she loved her parents, but she needed more than a room of her own—she needed her own place. She wondered if she'd ever feel at home in Southern California. She went on and on with details of her life that were overwhelming her at the moment. I walked over and put my arms around her, patting her back.

I put the mugs of tea aside and brewed a fresh pot of tea. "What we need are china tea cups and saucers," I announced. "These mugs will never do!"

I poured Marla's tea into a beautiful yellow chintz teacup. Getting my own favorite teacup and saucer, I led her into the living room and settled us down into adjacent corners of the couch and love seat. Curling up, we continued our visit, but now I was *there*; I was in the moment. I hadn't been *aware* of Marla when she first walked in the door. Now I was "eating that cup of salt" with her. Our friendship was deepening by the moment as my friend and I connected in the moment of her need. We looked into the mirrors of each other's souls and realized that the empathy I gave and the empathy Marla received that day caused her burden to be a shared burden. No woman is an island if she has a friend.

I was taking time, too, to obey the instructions in the Holy Scriptures: "Rejoice with those who rejoice, and weep with those who weep" (Romans 12:15 NAS). It is very easy to laugh with friends, but it is also very necessary to weep with them when they sorrow or hurt.

After an hour of tea and empathy, Marla blew her nose and dried her tears. She thanked me for the tea and the listening ear and said it was really time for her to go. I embraced my friend and prayed that God would give her grace for each day as it unfolded.

When Marla walked out of my door that day

which had started out in such an ordinary manner, she had partaken of comfort and encouragement served up from my own soul—a fellow-traveler who had "walked a mile in her shoes"—someone who knew what Marla was experiencing. It was also one more step into a more intimate friendship between the two of us.

℘

I learned an important lesson that day: if we want to have a friend, we must be a friend. And to be a friend, one needs to be very intentional about the moment. Listen to a person's tone of voice; watch her body language. Is she discouraged? Is something being said that is not verbalized?

I multi-task through most of my days. When I read or when I'm on the phone, or doing housework, or even writing at the computer, I'm thinking about ten different things at once. But being a friend means you stop!—you stop and focus on that person for that moment. Listen to her; look into her eyes. Make heart contact. And offer a cup of tea in a fine, lovely china cup as you head for a quiet, comfortable corner to talk—just the two of you. The tea and empathy will be just what you both need, and for just a little while, you will keep the "world that is too much with us" at bay.

℘ *Reflect* ~ Do I have friends with whom I can be vulnerable and transparent? Do I have people in my life that I consider intimate friends? With whom can I bare my soul?

ə *Respond* ~ I will choose to let the hurtful things I've experienced give me a heart of empathy. I will give my-"self" to intimate friendships, and I will be a friend to others. I will choose to be tastefully transparent about testing and trials in my life if it will give others a sense of hope that they, too, can face new opportunities tomorrow.

ഇ

"God knows how much I love you and long for you with the tender compassion of Christ Jesus. I pray that your love for each other will overflow more and more, and that you will keep on growing in your knowledge and understanding. I want you to understand what really matters, so that you may live pure and blameless lives until Christ returns." (Philippians 1:8-10 NLT)

ഇ

"Since human life is a fragile and unstable thing, we have no choice but to be ever on the search for people whom we may love, and by whom we may be loved in turn, for if charity and goodwill are removed from life, all the joy is gone out of it."
(Cicero)

ഇ

My life shall touch a dozen lives before this
      day is done,
Leave countless marks for good or ill ere sets
      the evening sun;
So this the wish I always wish, the prayer I
      ever pray,
Let my life help the other lives it touches by
      the way."

(unknown author)

❧ Chapter Eight ❧

Angel of Hope

"A clay pot sitting in the sun will always be a clay pot. It has to go through the white heat of the furnace to become porcelain."
(Mildred Witte Stouven)

Let me tell you, dear reader, about our Novel Tea in December of 2002. It became a memory day that inscribed itself on my heart.

Instead of meeting in one of our homes that month, we made reservations at a tea house located at the edge of the Pacific Ocean in Southern California. The sun sparkling off the dancing waves in the distance, and the palm trees swaying with a lazy indolence in a light breeze belied the reality that it was winter.

For this particular Novel Tea, we read Richard Paul Evans' books, *The Christmas Box* and *The Timepiece*. We entered the rarified ambiance of the tea room clutching our books and the gifts we'd brought to give each other. We made ourselves comfortable and cozy as the server took our orders for tea. She brought a triple tier laden with a variety of dainty sandwiches, scones, and chocolate cups filled with lemon custard. It was delectable fare! As we sipped our tea and nibbled scones, we opened up the novels we'd read that month.

Richard Paul Evans had touched our hearts with his simple novels. The themes of love and death and forgiveness and redemption were replete in the story of a little girl named Andrea and a mother who loved her daughter dearly. When Andrea died tragically, each one of us wept along with Mary Ann, the brokenhearted mother. We crept with her to a grave each day as she mourned under the shadow of an Angel of Hope statue. When Andrea's mother offered forgiveness to the person who had caused her daughter's death, we stood on a hypothetical precipice and wondered if we would have the largeness of soul to forgive so freely. Reading portions of the book out loud, we shed tears at the poignant rendering of human experience.

As we continued discussing the two novels, the server discreetly replenished our empty pots of tea and brought pastries for dessert. Lettie said she finished reading *The Timepiece* in an airport terminal. As she read, a woman approached and asked her what she was reading. She showed her the book. The woman responded that she'd been watching Lettie's face as she read and said it must be a wonderful book to cause so much emotion. The book did indeed invoke a response; the pathos of the storyline moved us deeply. Several readers remarked on Evans' portraits of characters that had old-fashioned virtues such as honesty, commitment, and loyalty.

We refilled our cups with piping hot English breakfast tea and, eyes shining with love and tears and gayety, we brought out the gifts we had tucked under our chairs. We don't spend much on our presents for each other, but the little mementos we give reflect the friendship of our hearts. Every little pretty spoon, Christmas tree "tea" ornament, or slim volume of poetry I've received over the years remind me of the women who have become my friends. The richness of the gift is in the heart of the giver, not the gift itself.

The food, the tea, and the readings we selected seemed to go on and on. We didn't want the time to end. When the teapot was finally empty and our hunger and conversation were satisfied, I made an announcement. The day wasn't over! We were now going to drive to the Lake Forest Memorial Park. They looked at me. A cemetery? they were silently asking. Yes! An Angel of Hope statue had been dedicated at that site a few months before, and I wanted my fellow-readers to see a tangible reminder and witness of the poignant stories we had just read and discussed.

Richard Paul Evans' books made the Angel of Hope famous. Parents who had experienced the loss of a child contacted Evans after reading about Mary Ann and her little girl's death in *The Christmas Box* and *The Timepiece*. Where could they go to find the angel and commemorate their own child's death the way MaryAnn did in his stories? Sensitive to the aching request of so many parents, Evans commissioned a sculptor to make the angel. This particular statue is now one of several that are erected in different cemeteries throughout the country.

On September 28 of 2002, I stood on this piece of hallowed ground when the Angel of Hope was dedicated. The statue is a four-foot, three-inch bronze child with her arms and wings outstretched, anchored on a granite pedestal. The inscription on the base of the statue reads: *"Angel of Hope: Our Children—Loved, Missed, and Remembered."*

About three hundred parents whose children had died and other family members sat in silence that day under a somber September sky. Evans explained why he had written the two books that introduced the Angel of Hope to the world. This soft-spoken, humble man stood in a misting rain on the graves of children who had left this earth too soon. He related the experience of his own mother enduring the death of a child. We felt his empathy as he recounted a dream he had in which his mother's agony had been re-enacted. When he awakened, he felt an almost holy compulsion to write her story of grief.

As he described the context of the angel that appeared in his books, we shifted our gaze to the statue standing in front of us, arms spread wide, looking into the heavens. He explained the comfort that the angels afforded parents and relatives. He knew the unique pain that a child's death inflicted on a family, and their longing for a child to be remembered.

The organizers of this event arranged for each of us to commemorate our deceased child. We formed a single-file line that curled around the cemetery. An older couple shrouded with a quiet dignity stood behind me in the long line, their arms around each other. They looked like they could be in their late seventies. I turned, smiled at them, and asked them how old their child had been. They seemed to be grateful for the question as they answered in unison: their only child, Harold, had died over forty years before when he was only three days old.

"Hyaline membrane disease," they murmured. "The same disease that President Kennedy's baby died of."

My heart contracted. Dear people—dear parents—still very much in need of solidifying the fact that Harold was a reality; that for three days they had loved and known their child.

And I was remembering a winsome, rambunctious little boy with tousled blond hair—a little boy who regularly scraped holes in the knees of his jeans. One day he was romping through our house, cavorting with his brother and sister. The next day he was sick; two months later he died. Where do we take a loss like that and make any sense of it? On this day, I took it to an angel.

As we slowly approached the front of the line, we were handed a white carnation. One by one we approached the microphone stationed by the Statue of Hope, repeated our child's name to the solemn crowd, and placed our carnation at the base of the angel. When I finally arrived at the front of the line, I took the carnation and stood at the microphone for several seconds. As much as I wanted to say the name of my son, "David James Chapman," I couldn't speak. I laid my flower at the base of the angel and moved on.

To the elderly parents behind me in line that day, their child's death was as recent as yesterday. My David was still very much my little boy even though he had died more than twenty years before when he was not yet six years old. Ah me, I thought, the grieving packed into all of the people gathered here together around this angel. Our children had been remembered, and we were gratified that something tangible and solid marked their reality and that their names had been heard.

Richard Paul Evans stood silent watch with us in the rain that day and continued to stand as he autographed our books. With his empathy, with his written words, with the commissioning of the Angel of Hope, he seemed to echo the sentiment of our souls: "I shall be richer all my life for this sorrow."[6]

Now as I stood here with my Novel Tea friends, I told them about the statue's dedication, and the tears that had anointed this hallowed ground. I told them about a baby named Harold

---

[6] Stegner, Wallace. *All the Little Live Things*. New York: Penguin Books. 1967. 345.

who died before he ever really had a chance to live. We were silent as the wind whispered around us. Inspecting the right wing of the angel, we found the word "Hope" that the sculptor had etched into his work. We read the inscription on the base of the Angel. Just as Andrea and Mary Ann had become real to us as we read Evans' fictional novels, the reality of his characters seared our consciousness as we gazed out over hundreds of stones marking the graves of children.

In the hushed atmosphere of the cemetery, Brenda remarked that the novels we had read reminded her how precious and fleeting the moments are that we have with our children as they grow. That very morning she had climbed into bed with Paul. It was pajama day in his class at school. She snuggled with him and thought about how cozy it was to have a moment with her son before the day started.

This juncture now for our Novel Tea members was the apex of our day. We had sipped and eaten and celebrated; however, this Angel was the tangible reminder that even though we had read fiction, the reality of life was represented right here in this memorial park. Our time together was over, but we would never forget the day or the books that introduced us to the Angel of Hope.

∞

I relate the story of this whole wonderful, emotion-packed, thought-provoking day to you, dear reader, so you can see how meaningful a Novel

Tea day can become. Friendships grow a little more divine when emotions are stirred and shared—when friends have "eaten a cup of salt" together. The common experience of tears *and* laughter braids the strands of friendship into an even tighter, thicker cord that cannot be broken.

ॐ   *Reflect* ~ What sorrows have I bottled up that only God knows about? Are the experiences caused by my losses making me "all the richer for having known them," or am I withering away in bitterness?

ॐ   *Respond* ~ I will ask God to reach down into the broken, sorrowing places of my life and pull me back up into the land of the living. I will look around with eyes of empathy and find those wounded souls that I can encourage to walk beside me on the road of healing and recovery.

ॐ

"Look! The home of God is now among his people! He will live with them, and they will be His people. God himself will be with them. He will remove all of their sorrows, and there will be no more death or sorrow or crying or pain. For the old world and its evils are gone forever." (Revelation 21:3-4 NLT)

ॐ

O God, whose laws will never change,
We thank Thee for these things we
    know;
That after rain the sun will shine;
That after darkness, light appears;
That winter always brings the spring;
That after sleep, we wake again;
That life goes on and love remains,
    And life and love can never die.

(Jeanette E. Perkins)

(For information about the Angel of Hope, please
visit this website:
www.careandkindness.org/angelofhope)

Chapter Nine

The Children's Tea Hour

"A whisper and then a silence, / Yet I know by their merry eyes / They are plotting and planning together / To take me by surprise."
(*from* "The Children's Hour"
by Henry Wadsworth Longfellow)

    A few years ago someone sent me a birthday card with a tea motif. Darling instructions were printed on the inside of the card about the proper way to go to a tea party:

"How to go to a Tea Party"
by Kitt Macy, Age 9

1. Wear a sutibul dress or skirt never pants or shorts.
2. Don't you ever go on Tuesdays or Friday the 13th.
3. Sip slowly, don't slurp.
4. Be jolly, laugh and eat at least 1 cookie.
5. Make an instring conversation.
6. Thank the host or hostist.

7. Give them at least 1 $.
8. After 5 times in a row the 6th time give a present.
9. Go again at least once.
10. Don't go and get things the host will bring it to you.
11. Have a great time!

I was thoroughly charmed and amused by the tea ritual as seen through the eyes of a nine-year old.

Brenda Green's daughters, Jocelyn and Charisse, have shown me what a tea ritual can be like when children are in charge. They had often helped their mom prepare for Novel Tea when it was her turn to host us at her house. They put their heads together to look over recipes and help their mom think out loud about what to serve. They even like to help her select which dishes and tea cups to use.

Once upon a time, however, these two girls put on their very own tea. And they were just about the same age as the little girl who wrote the instructions above on how to go to a tea. Jocelyn and Charisse did far more, though; they actually put on a tea for some little friends.

At the beginning of February a few years ago, Brenda talked to her girls about company that would be coming from Boston to stay with them. The couple's six-year-old daughter, Ella, would be with them. Brenda's kids absorbed their parents' excitement at the upcoming visit.

"Let's plan a Valentine's Tea Party for Ella," announced ten-year-old Jocelyn.

Charisse, eight years old, liked the idea. Tossing her long hair, she chimed in, "Yeah, let's plan a tea party with games and everything."

The two girls immediately got out paper and pencils and began making a guest list. "Who should we ask besides Ella?" they asked their mother.

Brenda wisely suggested they invite only four or five younger girls from their church since her girls were, after all, only eight and ten. They decided on another six year old, a little girl who was almost four, an *almost* three year old, and of course Ella. That would make six girls sitting around the table. "Just right!" pronounced Charisse.

Brenda went shopping with her daughters. They chose purple, pink, and red paper plates and napkins with teddy bears. They bought red mylar, heart-shaped balloons to tie on the back of each girl's chair. They decorated the entire den and dining room and the living areas with teddy bears and hearts to carry out their theme.

The girls sent out invitations that pictured little girls having a tea party with their dolls. Spinning off that picture, Jocelyn and Charisse asked each guest to bring her favorite doll or teddy bear and to wear either pink or red to the party.

With the party two weeks away, the girls now planned their activities. Brenda cautioned them to keep it simple since they had two very young girls. They wanted to have a "heart" scavenger hunt right in their own living room. Jocelyn and Charisse traced hearts on red and purple construction paper and cut them out. They carefully hid the cards in obvious places so it would be easier for little girls to find them. For a craft, the girls lined a long table on the patio with red and white checked paper cloth. They laid lavender construction paper down on top of that with glitter glue pens and sequins. They planned for each girl to be as creative as she wanted in making her own valentine.

(After the party, Brenda developed pictures that she had taken of each little girl at the Tea. She glued the picture of each girl to the valentine she had designed, laminated it, and gave it to the girl as a keepsake of the party. Great idea!)

The night before the party, the girls set the table and did the final decorating. Even though they used paper plates on which to eat, they put ceramic heart-shaped plates on Brenda's three-tiered server for the tea sandwiches. And what kind of sandwiches did they make? Peanut butter and jelly on white bread, of course! After they made the sandwiches, they cut them into heart shapes with a cookie cutter. They bought Little Debbie's heart cakes in pink and chocolate. When everything was arranged on the tiers, it looked exactly the way Jocelyn and Charisse had envisioned it—delicate and pink and very Valentine-y.

The BIG DAY finally arrived! It was February 14, Valentine's Day. The girls rushed home from school and made their final preparations. Even though Jocelyn and Charisse like to drink tea—especially with their mother!—they decided that little girls might like raspberry lemonade better. They put ice in the ceramic tea mugs and filled the Valentine teapot with lemonade. The table looked romantic and red balloons floated in the air above each chair.

At the appointed time, each guest arrived with her mommy. Jocelyn and Charisse led the guests down the hall to their bedroom. Each little girl got to choose her own hat, boa, and gloves, high heels, and jewelry from the dress-up trunk. They each sat at the table with their special doll or teddy bear. What a picture! The mommies hovered in the den and occasionally ventured close enough to take pictures. Brenda stood nearby in the kitchen just close enough to be of help in case her girls called her. The girls did the serving and made sure their little guests were comfortable. When a lull in the conversation occurred, Brenda would hear Jocelyn ask, "And what is the name of your teddy bear?" and the girls were soon chattering again.

The scavenger heart hunt went smoothly. Every little girl found hearts and brought them to Jocelyn for a prize. And Brenda said the sight of six darling little girls huddled over a table making their own valentines was a sight to behold. They cut and glued and wrote love messages that were an artist's delight! All in all, the party was a huge success. Brenda reported to all of us in Novel Tea that this was a real confidence-booster for her girls. And that was just their first Valentine's Tea Party. They have organized and hosted several teas over the years.

Brenda is another one of my heroines. She begins every day with moments of solitude in her "prayer closet" corner of her living room.

Sipping tea, she spends those moments absorbing God's Word and talking with Him. As her girls have grown into beautiful young women, they too, enjoy a cup of tea with Mom before they go to school. Brenda has the teapot on as they get dressed for school. Then as they sit at the kitchen table, the three of them chat as they drink tea together.

Brenda is training up her children by example and by hands-on teaching and mothering. As her children have grown, they have watched their mother using her gift of hospitality. They bask in the nurturing atmosphere of discipline, love, and the age-appropriate responsibilities they have been given since they were small children. And God is the center of their family and their home. It is a place of peace and calm. God bless the Green family.

ᔎ *Reflect* ~ What am I modeling to my children about my daily habits and rituals? Am I training them and instilling a desire for hospitality in their hearts? Do they see that I care for my soul during quiet times of reflection and reading?

ᔎ *Respond* ~ I will be much more aware of the life that I'm living in front of my watching children. I will endeavor to make my home a sanctuary for our family so that peace can be found within our walls.

"You must love the LORD your God with all your heart, all your soul, and all your strength. And you must commit yourselves wholeheartedly to these commands I am giving you today. Repeat them again and again to your children. Talk about them when you are at home and when you are away on a journey, when you are lying down and when you are getting up again. Tie them to your heads as a reminder, and wear them on your forehead. Write them on the doorposts of your house and on your gates." (Deuteronomy 6:5—9 NLT)

ℰℴ

"The home should be to the children the most attractive place in the world, and the mother's presence should be the greatest attraction." (Ellen G. White).

❧ Chapter Ten ❧

Tea by the Sea . . . Just Annie and Me

*"My precious daughter . . . I look into your
eyes and see the great wonder of God's
gift to me: a daughter to sing, laugh,
and have tea with."* (Jean Chapman)

I picked up my daughter at her little house
around noon on a Friday in May just a few short
years ago. She lived 125 steps from the ocean with
two other girls in a narrow little shoebox. They
just barely had room for the three of them, a few
pieces of furniture, and their surfboards.

Annie and I were on our way to Santa
Barbara. I had a speaking engagement the next
day, and the pastor's wife had graciously invited
my daughter to accompany me. Annie was only too
glad to get away for a couple of days. Studies and
some troubles of the heart were weighing on her.
She needed a change of scenery. And I needed to be
with my daughter!

Annie had been seeing a man that loved her;
however, my husband and I worried from a
distance that Matt loved her too much. He seemed

obsessed with our daughter. I hadn't seen her since we'd celebrated her 28th birthday just a month before. I was hoping that perhaps we would have some time to talk on this trip.

We drove the San Diego freeway up toward the 101 and wended our way through Los Angeles and the San Fernando Valley. We were like two birds flying north, away from our cages. Spring rustled through our beings like a fever. The day was balmy and lovely.

Annie chatted about her boyfriend. I listened and drove. We talked about her classes and some future dreams. We passed through Oxnard and headed toward Ventura.

"Mom, can I tell you about my week-end up in the mountains?" Annie asked. The afternoon sun glistened on the face of the ocean in the distance.

I listened as my daughter told me about a solitary retreat she had taken in order to spend some time with God. Over the years I had come to deeply appreciate Annie's thoughtful, contemplative nature. She was on her own personal journey, and she reflected independent thinking and a spirituality that marked her as a seeker and a traveler. She was also very much her own person, evolving and *becoming* the woman God was shaping her into. While she talked about her time alone up in the mountains, she took a folded packet of notebook paper out of her purse. Unfolding the sheet, I could see she had written on every line on both sides of the paper.

111

"Mom, I prayed and asked God to show me exactly what I should do about Matt. As I prayed, I felt like God showed me the qualities and attributes I should look for in a husband and not to settle for anything less. I wrote everything down on this paper."

She described her long walks up in the mountains, the times of prayer, the reading God had directed her to. I marveled at the hearing heart God had given my daughter.

I glanced over at Annie as she cleared her throat and prepared to read. Her blue eyes were very serious, and her long blonde hair partly veiled her tanned face from me.

Holding the paper in both hands, ducking her head a little to read, she started reciting the characteristics she wanted in a man—in a godly husband. After reading her list, she folded up her paper and told me that the man that came into her mind was Clarke.

"He has almost all of those attributes, Mom."

"Clarke?" I asked. "The guy you dated five years ago?"

"Yeah. When I wrote every single one of these qualities that God wants me to look for in a man, it dawned on me that Clarke is the guy who has all of those qualifications."

I didn't know Clarke. I didn't even know his last name. All I vaguely remembered was that Annie had been in love with a "Clarke" five years before when she was living with us and going to school. She was teaching at a Christian pre-school, and Clarke was on the pastoral staff. Excitedly one night, she told Larry and me that Clarke had organized a mission trip to Costa Rica for the church, and she was going.

When she came home from that trip, her face glowed when she talked about Clarke. She told us that Clarke had baptized her in the ocean along with other converts. Her recent conversion to Christ was made more significant by her baptism in water. And Clarke was the one who had baptized her!

And then one day there were tears on Annie's face. She didn't talk too much about Clarke anymore. He had made some changes in his life and moved to northern California. I had never even met him, but I sensed my daughter's deep unhappiness. Now she was telling me that this man named Clarke met all the requirements of a godly husband.

We drove a few more miles. The ocean was getting closer. I had a surprise for my girl that she didn't know anything about.

"Can we stop at Starbucks in Ventura, Mom?" my daughter asked.

I grinned at my daughter. "No. We'll stop a little farther up the way." She gave me a puzzled look. I could tell she was wondering what in the world I was up to!

We were going to stop, but not for coffee. That morning I had packed a picnic basket full of tea items. My burgundy teapot, two of my prettiest teacups and saucers, and a matching cream and sugar set were nestled in the basket with wads of paper towels stuffed around them. I put half-and-half in a small jar zipped into a baggie full of crushed ice. I added sugar and honey packets, Pepperidge Farm shortbread cookies, and tea bags in the basket. The last thing I did was put boiling hot water into a large thermos.

Now, with Annie watching me curiously, I guided the car slowly into unfamiliar territory. I had never been in this area of Ventura before, but I could see the ocean in front of me. There must be an accessible beach here somewhere.

"Where are we going, Mom? Why couldn't we get coffee back there at Starbucks?"

I smiled at her mysteriously and kept on driving. Spying the tops of palm trees a little to the west, I turned the wheel hoping that I was heading to a beautiful stretch of sand. God must have been hearing the anxious thoughts of my heart. I pulled into a parking lot at a perfect stretch of sandy beach. The sun was about half an hour from setting, palm trees swayed in the late afternoon breeze, and the beach was almost deserted. Delighted (thank you, God!), I parked the car. Annie's expressions registered how strange she thought this whole incident was becoming.

"What *are* you doing, Mom?"

"Just wait," I told her. "Come and help me get something out of the trunk."

As I reached into the trunk and lifted out the basket, I finally explained to Annie what we were going to do.

"We're going to have tea by the sea," I told my wondering daughter.

Annie whooped and hollered as she skipped over to the beach. "My mom and I are going to have tea by the sea!" she sang in a sing-song voice. "Hooray for Mom!"

We carefully spread a cross-stitched, embroidered linen cloth on the sand. Annie's eyes grew bigger as I took out my china teapot, the china cups and saucers, and the accessories. I poured the steaming hot water from the thermos into the pot and poked the teabags into the water. Soon Earl Grey tea was steeping to the desired strength. The last thing I took out of the basket was a votive candle. I lit the candle, put dainty cookies on a flowered porcelain plate, and *voilá,* we were ready for tea by the sea . . . just Annie and me!

Annie clasped her hands in front of her and beamed. "Did you bring a camera, Mom?"

"Of course I did." I held the camera out to her. "Find someone to take our picture together."

Annie danced over to a lone couple walking toward us and gave them a brilliant smile as she handed them the camera. "Would you take our picture, please? My mom and I are having tea on the beach!"

The couple gave us delighted smiles and snapped our picture.

My 28-year-old Annie was five years old again that day, and I was just "mommy" as we sipped our tea and let the wind blow through our hair. Boyfriend troubles, studies, and my speaking engagement the next day were far away. As the sun set on the horizon of the ocean, I realized that God had designed our day. Mother and daughter grasping a moment together in the landscape He had painted. It was a perfect moment, and it would be a memory that would last always.

Later that day, we checked into a charming old hotel in downtown Santa Barbara. As we walked down the main thoroughfare by our hotel and dawdled in a couple of quaint little boutiques, I marveled at this young woman who was beautiful and godly and who deeply desired a husband that God had waiting for her. I thought back to a couple of years before when Annie had crawled into my bed at night, crying, asking me if I thought she would ever get married and have children. She had been a bridesmaid for several friends; beautiful gowns hung side by side in her closet. Would she ever be the bride? The one who was celebrated at bridal showers? The one who would walk down an aisle, dressed in a long white gown, to meet a man who stood center stage waiting for her?

I pulled her close to me and hugged her, wiping the tears off her cheeks.

"Oh, yes. God has someone for you. In fact, he's somewhere out there right now calling, 'Annie, Annie. Where are you, Annie?' He just doesn't know where you live yet," I reassured my girl.

After that wonderful week-end in Santa Barbara, Annie and I returned home to studies, school, and jobs. Some time went by, and my husband and I became aware that Annie and Matt were no longer seeing each other. We breathed a prayer of thanks to God for His intervention. Almost a year later, Annie gave me a follow-up to the story that began that serendipitous Mother-Daughter weekend.

A couple of weeks after our Santa Barbara trip in May of 2001, Clarke left a message on Annie's answering machine. She returned his call, they talked a little bit and met for coffee a couple of times; however, Annie was tenuous about starting a relationship with Clarke. After all, his track record had been a little inconsistent in the past! And she had come to a point of contentment in her singleness. So she guarded her heart and set some boundaries.

A year went by. We were making plans to go to the mountains for Thanksgiving. Our son, Scott, had married Danielle in July of 2002. The newlyweds would be going with us to the condo. Annie called Larry just a few days before the holiday.

"Dad, can I bring a guy with me to the mountains for Thanksgiving?" she asked.

"Well, of course you can," Larry responded. "What's his name?"

Annie answered, "His name is Clarke, Dad, and he's just *wonderful!*"

We smiled as we wondered who this *wonderful* guy was. We were anxious to meet Clarke.

When Clarke and Annie walked in the door of our condo up in the mountains on Thanksgiving evening, Larry and I knew that this was the guy. There was a connection between the two of them that was almost tangible. When Annie introduced him to us, something clicked in my brain when she said she had known him years before. This was *that* Clarke!

After we had made all the introductions, we settled down in the living room to chat for a little while before dinner needed tending. Clarke seemed at ease with all of us, and Annie sat beaming beside him on the couch. I finally broached the question Larry and I had on our minds.

"Where have you been for six years?" I asked with one eyebrow arched and a rather stern smile on my face.

He endeared himself to me immediately with his disarming candor.

"Jeanie," he began explaining earnestly, "it wasn't God's timing for me or Annie six years ago. I wasn't the man I needed to be for Annie, and God had plans for Annie, too." I wondered what he meant by all that, but it wasn't the time nor the place to start an interrogation.

He continued his story as he briefly described his own journey—his move to northern California, working at Mt. Hermon by Santa Cruz and attending seminary. Annie and Clarke held hands as he talked, and she smiled at him in a way that melted my heart.

Annie grinned at me. "Do you want to interview Clarke, Mom?" I was puzzled. Why would she ask me to do that?

She proceeded to describe her meeting with Clarke's mom and dad just a few days before. Clarke told Annie he wanted to run by his folks' house so they could meet her. However, when they arrived at the home of Clarke's parents, Yoli Brogger, Clarke's beautiful dark-haired mom, had a formal tea waiting to serve. Handsome, warm, loving Bob Brogger had a blazing fire roaring in the fireplace.

"Mom, Yoli served tea and heart-shaped scones, and they asked me all kinds of questions," Annie grinned with impudence at Clarke and continued her story.

"Mom—they're wonderful! I think they like me, and I love them! But . . . don't you think you should interview Clarke, Mom?"

I didn't want to "interview" Clarke just then. There was a turkey to carve and a table to set; however, I watched and I listened throughout the rest of the day. I very much wanted this to be someone who would cherish my daughter and respect her mind and her heart. In the next few hours, it became apparent that Clarke had a deep love for God and that he loved our daughter. He was respectful of both of us and extremely courteous. I wondered if this wasn't just possibly the man that God had reserved in the wings all these years for our daughter.

Annie finished all of her course work for her Masters in Clinical Psychology at Vanguard University just before Christmas that year. The following February, Clarke had chosen the day and the place where he would ask our daughter to marry him. At one point, he had asked Annie what her idea of a perfect proposal would be.

She thought for a moment; then she told him that her idea of a perfect setting for a marriage proposal should have the elements of family, the ocean, poetry, and music. And so the man who would become our son-in-law planned the proposal. He told Annie to block out the Saturday following Valentine's Day—just to be ready for a day on the beach.

Friends who had a little cottage right on the beach at El Moro in Laguna gave permission for Clarke to use their vacation home. Bob and Yoli arranged food and deep red, stemmed goblets and sparkling cider for toasting the newly-engaged couple on the veranda that sat on the edge of the ocean. Larry and I, Bob and Yoli, and Clarke's and Annie's best friends waited on the wooden deck.

Clarke had cued his buddies. Arranging a picnic on the sand for the two of them, he planned a long stroll down the beach. Clarke's friend was high above them on a bluff taking pictures of the two of them meandering, eating, and stopping for an occasional kiss. Their destination—unbeknownst to Annie—was the cottage where we all waited, hiding and peeking at them as they slowly made their way toward us. Another friend hid behind a lattice by the portico of the little house ready to videotape the proposal. Three friends with guitars stood on the veranda ready to serenade the couple as they approached the cottage.

The sun flitted in and out of clouds that scuttled across the afternoon sky. We watched Clarke and Annie from our vantage point; they were specks in the distance. They came closer. We could make out Clarke's tall, lanky figure and Annie's slender shape beside him, blond hair blowing in the wind. We saw Clarke stop and bend over. Yoli explained excitedly that Clarke had written a long poem about his love for Annie and placed it in a bottle that he had partially buried in the sand. We could see Clarke holding a paper, facing Annie and reading to her. Then we saw her crying and the two of them melded into one silhouette as they held each other with the sun suspended in the sky behind them.

They came closer to the cottage. We dashed

inside and peeked through the mini-blinds to watch the rest of the drama unfold. Scott and Joel and Tim started singing John Denver's "Annie's Song" as our kids walked up to the romantic little cottage nestled in the sand.

"Look who's here and singing your song, Annie," Clarke said grinning with delight at our enraptured daughter.

The two of them walked up onto the deck. The three singers finished their song, bid the lovebirds adieu, and took off. Annie sat down on a little bench facing the window. Clarke knelt down in front of her with his back to us. We all watched and held our breath. This was it! Clarke was proposing marriage to Annie! My heart was trembling.

We could see that Clarke was reading something, and Annie kept nodding her head, smiling at Clarke and touching his face. We learned later that Clarke was reading scriptures to Annie that spoke about the word "always"—"We always carry around in our body the death of Jesus, so that the life of Jesus may also be revealed in our body" (2 Corinthians 4:10); "So I strive always to keep my conscience clear before God and man" (Acts 24:16). He read several more verses, and Annie sat facing this young man with the sun dropping lower and lower in the afternoon sky. Finally Clarke asked that very important question. As he slid the ring on our daughter's finger, we drew the blinds up, applauded wildly and dashed out to congratulate the just-engaged couple.

Later, when the hugging was over, when the parents had calmed down, when the toasts had been made to the couple standing before us, Clarke made a little speech, his arm around Annie's waist.

"Thank you all for being here on this stormy, sunny day," he began in poetic fashion. Sure enough, at just that moment, late-afternoon February clouds parted and a ray of sunshine fell softly on the heads of our children spreading a halo of light around them. It was as though God was giving His personal benediction to our whole family. Bob Brogger led in a prayer of blessing over Clarke and Annie and we felt the kiss of God on the faces of our children.

Clarke and Annie were engaged to be married in February. She celebrated her thirtieth birthday in April, graduated with her M.S. in Clinical Psychology in May, and got married in June. The year was 2003. God had indeed reserved just the right man for our Annie that in His sovereignty was the soul-mate she had waited for. And our daughter was the wife that Clarke had been searching for—everything simply had to be done in God's good timing for their lives.

And here's an interesting footnote to this romantic tale that we learned after the engagement: Clarke and Annie didn't have an actual "date" until almost a year after the message he left on Annie's phone a couple of weeks after she and I had been to Santa Barbara. After that first real date—a nice dinner and evening together—

Clarke drove Annie back to her little shoebox of a house in Newport. He walked her to the door.

"Annie, can we pray together before you go in?" he asked her.

She thought that felt very *right* for them to do.

Several weeks later they were eating at a little health food restaurant in Corona del Mar. Clarke impulsively slapped the table and with great intensity, he asked her, "Annie Chapman, will you be my exclusive girlfriend?"

It was at that moment that Annie remembered some specific items she had written in her journal some time before. They were both astonished when she told Clarke about her entries. "I want the man I'm supposed to marry to pray with me before he says 'Good-bye' after our first date," she wrote. "I want the man I fall in love with to tell me by the fourth date that he wants me to be his exclusive girlfriend." She had written those details almost with a "Ha-ha" attitude—"That'll never happen!"

But the God who writes the scripts to our lives was perhaps smiling and saying "Ha-ha," also. You see, Annie had come to a point in her life when she was very content with who she was; she was very content with her single status in life. God had been her provider, her "husband" just as the Word promised He would be. She evidenced a very healthy sense of self-awareness that didn't necessarily need a man to define her. God and

Annie had done that defining in a divine partnership.

Now—over two and a half years after our daughter's wedding—Clarke sits beside Annie at our table as we break bread together, and he is indeed our son. We love Annie and Clarke and they honor us and love us. We thank God for our incredible, wonderful daughter, our son-in-law and his family who have opened their arms to us and drawn us into the heart of their family.

ॐ

God gave Annie and me that moment in time on that particular day in May in 2001. It didn't just happen, however. That morning I had been very purposeful as I read my Bible and spent time in prayer. I had asked God to breathe some ideas into my mind and heart about making my time with Annie memorable. As I got busy packing and getting ready for our weekend trip, little pieces of the overall "tea by the sea" plan came to me. I was excited as I started packing my basket with tea things. And then I had a mental picture painted across my mind of the two of us sitting on a beach by the ocean. Pretty soon the plan was designing itself in its entirety. When I actually pulled it off later that day, I was more excited than Annie.

It would be so easy to use some creativity and plan similar outings with your children or grandchildren. Take just one child with you or several. You could replicate Tea by the Sea by having Tea at the Park, a tailgate tea party at a ballpark stadium, or simply sit on the grass in your back yard and plan a quiet time of tea and conversation. Your little darlings (and your bigger darlings, too!) will love being alone with you and having your full attention. So make the most of those unexpected moments and plan a tea in God's great outdoors with someone you love.

---

୬ *Reflect* ~ Have I allowed God to reign over my life with His divine sovereignty? Where do I see evidence of God's grand design in my life?

୬ *Respond* ~ I will surrender my calendar, my schedule, my loved ones to God. I will allow God to use me in ways He sees fit to encourage other people through my acts of service. I will encourage my children to seek God's will for their own lives in everything they do.

"Children are a gift from the LORD; they are a reward from him. Look at all those children. There they sit around your table as vigorous and healthy as young olive trees. That is the LORD's reward for those who fear him." (Psalm 127:3 & 128:3-4 NLT)

∞

"My child, you leave my home but not my heart. Your years in my care have blessed me as I have watched the unfolding of your life. It is with pride and tenderness that I now release that life to follow its own promise. I love you. I believe in you. I wish only the best for you." (Noela N. Evans in *Meditations for the Passages and Celebrations of Life*)

❧ Chapter Eleven ❧

A Tisket, a Tasket, Our Tea is in the Basket

"She has taken her bright candle and is gone into another room I cannot find, but anyone can tell where she has been by all the little lights she leaves behind."
(unknown author)

Have you ever noticed that there are those people who illuminate our lives simply by their influence? There's an aura that is projected from them; a persona that makes one want to linger in their presence. Ruth was one of those people. She had a strong voice, she was a mighty preacher; she was Shakespearean in her vocal delivery when she quoted long passages of the Bible from memory. No one who ever heard her speak forgot her. She was a personality as sharp and strong as a multi-faceted diamond. In her day, she was a tremendous teacher and a great personality.

But the inevitable happened. Ruth got older. Her memory wasn't quite as sharp as it had once been. She fell and bones broke. Getting older and infirm wasn't her cup of tea. Ruefully, she told me one day to enjoy life now because it didn't get any better as you got older. Ah . . . the light was growing dimmer; she was wandering into another room. Her memory was fading along with her vitality.

Ruth had been married to an Englishman. He was also a minister and together, the two of them became legendary as they led lives of stellar service in God's great kingdom. She had learned to make a proper pot of tea—by osmosis, she seemed to become British also. In her glory days, she reigned over her teatime dispensing tea with lumps of sugar and slices of lemon. And the variety of her teapots and teacups was a wonder to behold. She had collected them from all over the world during her lifetime.

Ruth had impacted my life greatly during those times I heard her speak. And so one day, Lynora (my Novel Tea friend) called to tell me she was on her way to visit Ruth. She had fallen— again!—and was in a convalescent hospital. When Lynora asked me if I wanted to go with her to see Ruth, I accepted the invitation enthusiastically.

"Let's take tea things and serve tea when we go to see her," I suggested.

And so I packed my picnic basket once again with all my tea goodies. Lynora picked me up, and we were off to spend time with this very special lady.

Ruth was a little out of sorts when we walked into her room. She eyed the basket I carried with unfeigned curiosity, however. Lynora hugged her and greeted her brightly. Lynora—

dear, dear Lynora—has the gift of bright chatter
and brighter smiles as she quickly and efficiently
gets things accomplished. Within seconds, she had
Ruth sitting up and had her putting her shoes on.
She scooted her into a chair by the hospital bed.
Then she fluffed up her hair. Ruth's shoulders
were straightening up. She was still eyeing my
basket.

"You know what we're going to do?" asked
Lynora cheerfully.

"What?" she asked rather brusquely.

"We're going to have tea!" Lynora had her
fun voice on. Her infectious enthusiasm made it
seem as though we were little girls planning a tea
party.

Meanwhile I spread a linen cloth over the
hospital table by Ruth's bed. I poured the boiling
water from the thermos into my grandmother's
burgundy teapot and let the Earl Grey tea bags
steep for awhile. Then I brought out the crystal
sugar and creamer set, poured half-and-half from a
jar into the creamer, and poured sugar from a zip-
lock baggie into the sugar container. The narrow
table was beginning to look beautiful as I placed
the napkins and teacups alongside the teapot.

After putting the shortbread cookies on a
porcelain plate, I announced that I was ready to
serve tea.

"Which cup would you like, Ruth?" Lynora
asked our friend.

Ruth's piercing eyes examined each cup
carefully. Finally she pointed to the Elizabethan

Staffordshire fine bone china cup painted with full-blown hot-pink roses.

I poured tea for all of us. Ruth sipped her tea and responded as Lynora chatted with her about old times; mutual friends they both knew, places Ruth had lived, and Ruth's adored grand-daughter, Heather. We were interrupted for a moment by a nurse who stopped in the doorway to greet our friend.

"You've got company, Ruth. How nice!"

Ruth looked at her for a moment, then nodded assent. She was a queen holding court once again.

Arching her eyebrows, she responded imperiously, "We're having high tea!" And with that, she continued sipping.

We enjoyed our teatime immensely with Ruth that day. Although she never commented specifically, she seemed slightly amazed that we not only would, but that we could bring tea to her. We were gratified that the simple ritual of serving tea and the ensuing conversation had been enough to brighten Ruth's spirits and give her a moment from the past. We took tea to her a couple more times until she was mended enough to return to her apartment.

Ruth's once brightly burning candle grew dimmer and dimmer until it was snuffed out by death in 2003. It is heartening, however, to see the glowing candles of incandescence that her daughter and grand-daughter and even her great-grandchildren radiate. Ruth is a reminder to me that one generation lights the candles of the generation walking on the path behind them. Ruth has "gone into another room," but even as she glowed brightly during her halcyon days, she was careful to lean over and light the candle of her daughter. Her daughter has been as diligent in lighting the candles of her children and grandchildren.

What a privilege to serve tea to Ruth! This woman shone as a stellar light to illuminate truths of God's Word for me at one time. Her influence will remain with me into eternity. Someone once wrote that "the good person increases the value of every other person whom she influences in any way." Ruth was that good person who gave value to everyone who sat within the radius of the light she cast. Only her family members can adequately tell Ruth's story. They are also remarkable people who cast a wide circle of brilliant light in their areas of ministry.

And now my friend Lynora packs up her basket and serves tea to a group of widows who meet together once a month. They were all married to ministers at one time. As they sip their tea, they visit and reminisce about the days when they shared the joys and the responsibilities of ministering alongside their husbands. But they still enjoy a genteel time of visiting and a good cup of tea. God bless all the women who hold their candles high and walk before us giving us light on the pathway of life!

Philip Yancey relates a story called "Young and Old" about this very real thing of aging: An elderly woman approached the former president of a Bible college, with the question: " . . . why [does] God let us get old and weak. 'Why must I hurt so?' After a few moments thought, [he] replied, 'I think God has planned the strength and beauty of youth to be physical. But the strength and beauty of age is spiritual. We gradually lose the strength and beauty that is temporary so we'll be sure to concentrate on the strength and beauty which is forever. It makes us more eager to leave behind the temporary, deteriorating part of us and be truly homesick for our eternal home. If we stayed young and beautiful, we might never want to leave!'"[7]

As women in today's society, let us be very careful to nurture and enhance the inner spirit that dwells within us; let us be cognizant of our future days and understand that what we are *becoming* today will be magnified as a product in our later years.

Cultivate the soul!

---

୬ *Reflect* ~ As I look back over my life, who are the women who have shone a light on my path? Who have influenced me for good? Do I value women who are walking ahead of me on the path of

---

[7] Yancey, Philip. *Stories of Hope for the Healthy Soul.* Zondervan Gifts. 1999. 114.

life? Women of wisdom and experience? What do I learn from them?

༄   *Respond* ~ I will light my candle and determine to be a bright influence in the lives of others while there is opportunity. I will seek relationship with those who have walked more miles on their path than I have on mine; women who can share their light with me. I will nurture my soul—today!

༄

"Gray hair is a crown of glory; it is gained by living a godly life." (Proverbs 16:31 NLT)

༄

"We are holding a light. We are to let it shine! Though it may seem but a twinkling candle in a world of blackness, it is our business to let it shine. We are kindling a fire. In this cold world full of hatred and selfishness our little blaze may seem to be unavailing, but we must keep our fire burning."
(Billy Graham)

Chapter Twelve

A Skid Row Tea

"If anyone gives you even a cup of water because you belong to the Messiah, I assure you, that person will be rewarded." (Mark 9:41 NLT)

Every December Millie, Judy, and I host a Christmas Tea for some of our heroines. Who are they? They are women who are missionaries, pastors, or ministers' wives. Since the three of us are married to the officials who oversee all of our pastors for Southern California, we feel as though we pastor these women; certainly we are aware of the unique blessings *and* stresses of their position. It is our purpose at these Christmas Teas to express our gratitude to each woman for her selflessness in ministering to the people God has placed in her life.

This particular day, the tea was held in my home. About 45 women crowded into every corner of the house and spilled out onto the patio. As I circulated with a pot of tea to refill empty cups, I heard snatches of conversations filtering through my home. Kay was telling about the last

Christmas gift, a baby carriage for her dolls, that her dying mother had given her when she was only nine years old. "I didn't know it was my last Christmas with her," she said wistfully.

In another corner, Gwendolyn talked about the time when she was a little girl and got exactly what she wanted for Christmas one year—a Dale Evans' cowgirl outfit complete with double-holster, cap-shooting guns. I smiled to hear Gwen's deep-throated laugh. Serving as a pastor alongside her husband, Jamal, in downtown Los Angeles, she has long-since put away her cap guns and was now wielding the sword of the Bible as her chief weapon of defense.

Candy was over on the couch talking to women sitting on the floor around her. She shared about the gunfire they heard in the streets almost every night outside their home in Lynwood. Very matter-of-factly she related how they dropped to the floor when the gunfire was close and they heard cars screeching by. They had gotten used to the sounds of the inner-city. I looked out the window at my wide, jacaranda-bordered street and realized Candy and Gwen may as well live in another country compared to Irvine.

Millie and Judy herded the women toward the living room as Sherry started playing the piano. I went to the kitchen to put some food away before I joined the others to sing Christmas carols. Linda captured me with her words and her expression as soon as I was alone by the sink.

"Do you think you could ever help me put on a tea like this for my women on Skid Row?" she asked. Her eyes were pleading and hopeful at the same time.

Hmmm . . . as a home missionary, I knew that Linda had raised her own support to go down into the bowels of Los Angeles. She felt that God had called her to start a church on Skid Row. Every Saturday night, with the help of volunteers, she went up and down alleys knocking on boxes and cardboard, offering people "beans, rice, and Jesus Christ." Over a period of time she had enough street people to start a church—most of them women and children.

I went to visit Linda. Her church was one street removed from the garment district where hordes of women planned all-day shopping sprees. It truly is the consumer capital of Southern California. The enclave of Skid Row might just as well be on another planet as one street removed from this shopping mecca.

When Linda took me across the street from her little store-front church to a huge hotel that housed many of these women and children, people called to her from every sidewalk, "Hi, Pastor Linda. Hey, Pastor!" I entered the old, hollowed-out hotel with Linda and heard loud echoes of children's voices screeching and reverberating under the dome high above. Going up and down hallways and peeking into rooms through open doors, I was appalled at the squalid conditions in which these women and children lived. A constant cacophony of noise pummeled us—voices yelling, televisions blaring, and honking cars and street sounds that penetrated through the walls of the hotel from the outside world.

Linda genuinely loved these people trapped in a world of poverty, violence, and hopelessness. Now she was asking me to help her put on a tea for her women and children. Of course I would help her! We looked at our calendars and settled on a date.

I knew I could not do this alone. I had several months before the tea was scheduled, however, so I prayed and asked the Lord to send me the help I needed. Once again I called my friend, Lynora. She was glad to be part of the tea team. Then I called my pastor's wife, Lenora, and she said I could have anything I needed from the church's decorating storeroom. I looked through the women's ministries assortment of centerpieces and selected small, round clear containers that looked like fishbowls. I had already decided I would cut hibiscus flowers the day before the tea; they would be lovely in the small bowls. Lenora also loaned me ten round white tablecloths from the church supplies.

A few weeks later, I attended a church picnic and met a family I had only seen on the other side of the sanctuary. They laid their blanket on the lawn right next to ours. I introduced myself to the pretty red-haired mom and found out her name was Judy. We made small talk for awhile. In passing I mentioned the tea I was going to put on in a couple of months for my friend on Skid Row.

"Do you need any help?" Judy asked. I looked at her pretty face and said, "Yes. I'd love to have any help you can give." I was to find out later that Judy was very creative and did the silk flower arrangements at church that I had admired so much.

There were only a couple more things that needed to be arranged. I wanted to have some sort of a program since we would have so many children coming to our tea. I called Robin, a Children's Pastor, and asked if she would come with her puppets and put on a show for us. She gave an enthusiastic "Yes!" My husband made up some flyers at the office with details about the tea. I mailed them to Linda, and she started handing them out up and down the sidewalks of Skid Row.

The week of the tea finally arrived. I went to Costco and Sam's Club and bought frozen finger foods, desserts, bottled punch, tea bags, and bags of crushed ice. I stored everything that was cold or frozen in my refrigerator and freezer. The finger foods were spiral ham and turkey sandwiches, hors d'oeuvres that were ready to eat as soon as they were defrosted, and bags of frozen fruit cut into bite-sized pieces. For dessert I bought miniature pecan tarts, cream puffs, and an assortment of fancy cookies. To make it as simple as possible, we were going to use service ware that could be thrown away: fluted plastic plates and fancy plastic cups with handles for our tea (or punch for the kids). We used plastic forks and spoons. Linda insisted that I save the receipts for the food; she wanted to pay for everything out of her mission budget. Everything we bought for the tea came to under $90—not bad for a tea to feed around 80 women and children!

Lynora and I cut beautiful pink hibiscus flowers from lush bushes in our neighborhood the day before our tea and put the flowers in water overnight.

The next morning, Judy and Lynora and I loaded up my van with all the supplies and food and ice chests. Since I had no idea if there was a kitchen or a sink in the building where we would be holding our tea, I filled a 100-cup coffeemaker (also borrowed from our church) with water at my house. I hoped that with the lid attached securely, the water wouldn't slosh out in my car. We drove out of Orange County and headed up the freeway to downtown Los Angeles.

When we arrived, it seemed as though we had entered a foreign country. Linda stood outside her store-front church watching for us. She pointed to the parking lot we were to pull into. Several of her volunteers came out and helped us unload the van. Round tables had been set up in her "sanctuary." With about an hour to go before the tea began, Judy, Lynora, and I kicked our energy into high gear. I had chosen the right women: they worked quickly and efficiently. They saw what needed to be done.

We were fortunate that Linda had a narrow room adjacent to the sanctuary. We worked and did all of our preparation there. As soon as Lynora had tablecloths on the tables, Judy came behind her with the round vases. She gently laid a hot-pink hibiscus flower in each container. She swirled silk ivy around the base of each vase in an artful manner. By the time we had burgundy napkins and plates and spoons and cups on each place setting, the tables looked very pretty and the hall was beginning to look very festive. The water was coming to the boiling point in the coffeemaker, and the three of us were arranging finger foods and desserts on crystal platters from our china hutches. Lynora and I also brought our most beautiful teapots from home in which to serve the tea.

Our food was ready to serve, and our teapots and pitchers of punch were ready to pour. Pam, a neighboring pastor's wife who had gladly volunteered to help us, stood at the front of the church with an assortment of hats donated from her women. As our guests began to arrive, they picked the hat they wanted to wear for our tea.

Linda seemed ready to burst with pride and joy as she welcomed each woman and child. She swirled around the room in her high heels and polka dot dress with a brilliant smile on her face. These were her people and she was their pastor. I was reminded of a quote I'd once read: "To find joy in another's joy, that is the secret of happiness." Linda was indeed happy, and she was igniting joy in her women and their children by giving them a formal tea.

Classical music played softly from the CD player I brought with me. Lynora, Judy, and I served the women. "Tea or punch?" Lynora asked brightly. Little girls' eyes got big at the fancy foods layered on the large platters. Hesitantly they reached out and carefully picked out one or two strange-looking, dainty spiral sandwiches. I whispered to Linda that the women looked so pretty in their summer dresses. She giggled and whispered back that she had taken the moms shopping at a Ross discount store.

"You wouldn't believe what it's like to take four and five women at a time from Skid Row shopping for dresses!" she exclaimed. But as I looked at them, all dressed up and wearing hats, I was proud of Linda. She knew that dressing up for a tea would heighten the experience for them.

Pastor Linda introduced the three of us to the women. Then she asked me to tell the group about our special guest, Pastor Robin. Robin came up to the front with her puppets and the rest of the day took care of itself. Even the older women were sitting on the edge of their seats as Robin introduced each of her puppets. I had seen her working at children's camps. Somehow she manages to tell a Bible story with extraordinary animation while she's talking to her puppet. She assumes voices for each character; they banter and screech back and forth at each other. Robin is one talented lady! At one point I looked over to the door that faced the street. Even though the door was open, the protective bars that covered the opening were tightly closed. Grizzled old men and women with weathered faces stood beside hardened teenagers on the other side of the bars listening to the stories Robin told. Their eyes were glued on the story-teller and her puppets. When she finished her program, she asked everyone to bow their heads as she prayed for them. Through her gift of drama and her form of storytelling, Robin had touched the hearts of these women and children with the Spirit of God.

When the tea was over, the women and children lingered, reluctant to leave this place. Judy and Lynora and I headed into the side room to begin cleaning up. Children followed us in a herd and put out eager hands for leftover cookies. Several women whispered shyly that they had other kids at home. Could they please take some food home for them? We wrapped up every bit of food that was left over in paper napkins and sent it home with women who crept back to their corners of Skid Row.

We were exhausted and sobered as we left
the world of downtown Los Angeles and drove back
to Orange County. Were we glad we had gone
down there to put on a tea? Absolutely! Would we
do it again? In a heartbeat. It took a two-day
commitment of time to shop for the supplies and
then actually spend one day putting on the tea.
But the value of that little bit of time to give
women and their daughters the experience of
dressing up and partaking of fancy food and tea
cannot be calculated. We helped Linda make
memories for her congregation that day. Perhaps
through something as special and as simple as
enjoying a tea party, some hearts were touched in a
manner that made an eternal impact on their souls.
What a blessing to give out of the abundance with
which God had blessed us.

I gave very specific details, dear reader, as I
wrote about the Tea on Skid Row. You can do the
same thing in your corner of the world. It does take

work and organization; it does take a team of people; it does take time. But if you're willing to work a little bit and leave your comfort zone for awhile, it can be done.

Every person is a human being imbued with a soul. I had spoken for these women a couple of times before I ever put on the Tea that Saturday on Skid Row. I've talked with these women. They seem to be imprisoned in the inner-city because of their economic status. But the hope for them, the hope for any of us, is Jesus Christ. He changes the heart and takes the slum out of the person.

These women spoke to me with heartbreak about the vast sea of social systems and red tape they navigated to get special help for their children. They were poor, they said, and at the mercy of "the system." I agreed with them. They were terribly concerned about their children and their children's future. I reminded them, however, that very wealthy women lived just a few blocks away up in the hills above them who had the same concerns about their children.

"They have plenty of money, they can afford counselors, their kids go to the best schools. And yet many of their children are on drugs; some commit suicide. Just having money doesn't take away the problem." I shared with them the purpose Jesus had in coming to this earth—the need we had for forgiveness of our sins; the need to have hope in order to live through desperate circumstances. I shared the scripture from the prophet Isaiah: *"Is this not the fast which I chose, to loosen the bonds of wickedness, to undo the bands of the yoke, and to let the oppressed go free, and break every yoke? Is it not to divide your bread with the hungry, and bring the homeless poor into the house; when you see the naked, to cover him?"* (Isaiah 58:6-7 NAS)

I shared Jesus' own words: *"It is not those who are healthy who need a physician, but those who are ill. But go and learn what this means, 'I desire compassion, and not sacrifice,' for I did not come to call the righteous, but sinners"* (Matthew 9:12-13 NAS). The women listened, some with tears, to God's Word that reassured them that He loved them and cared about them with a passion they perhaps had never heard about before.

I once read that when God looks at all of humanity, He sees individual faces. He doesn't see ideas or statistics. And our faces are not a nebulous blur to Him; they have specific features and expressions, and they are all colors. *"In each face a loving heavenly Father sees mirrored life's dreams and disappointments, life's pains and pleasures, life's work and worship. The more like God we become, the greater will be our concern about people"* (Pease, Norval F.).

God looked at my face and heart and *knew* me and my future before I was ever conceived (Psalm 139; Ephesians 1:4). He sees and knows the marginalized lives and desperation of the women on Skid Row. He gives us an internal hope that Jesus Christ ignites in our hearts when we give Him our lives. If giving even a cup of cold

147

water in the name of Jesus does not go unrewarded, then I pray that a cup of tea given by loving hands will leave an imprint of love on the ones who receive.

––––––––––

ও   *Reflect* ~ Have I considered the less fortunate in our society? Am I aware of the homeless women and children in our society? How does my life reflect compassion?

ও   *Respond* ~ I will make a contribution on some level to help those who are more unfortunate than I am—through prayer, making financial donations, or volunteering aid of some sort on a regular basis.

ഓ

"Pure and lasting religion in the sight of God our Father means that we must care for orphans and widows in their troubles, and refuse to let the world corrupt us. [. . .] what's the use of saying you have faith if you don't prove it by your actions? Suppose you see a brother or sister who needs food or clothing, and you say, 'Well, good-bye and God bless you; stay warm and eat well'—but then you don't give that person any food or clothing. What good does that do? I can't see your faith if you don't have good deeds." (James 1:27 & 2:14-18 NLT)

ഓ

I was hungry and you formed a humanities
club to discuss my hunger.
Thank you.
I was imprisoned and you crept off quietly to your
chapel to pray for my release.
Nice.
I was naked and in your mind you debated
the morality of my appearance.
What good did that do?
I was sick and you knelt and thanked God
for your health.
But I needed you.
I was homeless and you preached to me of
the shelter of the love of God.
I wish you'd taken me home.
I was lonely and you left me alone to pray
for me.
Why didn't you stay?
You seem so holy, so close to God; but I'm still very
hungry, lonely, cold, and still in pain.
Does it matter?

(Anonymous)

❧ Chapter Thirteen ❧

Grace for the Week

*"Since human life is a fragile and unstable thing, we
have no choice but to be ever on the search for people
whom we may love, and by whom we may be loved in
turn, for if charity and goodwill are removed from life,
all the joy is gone out of it."*
(Cicero)

I put my pen down and leaned back in my
chair. Not yet midnight, my husband, Larry, was
still at the church office refining his sermon for the
next morning. I was alone. Thoughts from the
week intruded on my lesson plans as I finalized my
own notes for tomorrow's Sunday School class.

The week had been exhausting. A myriad of
people had stumbled across my path. I felt the
immense need for God's grace and strength for the
days that had just gone by. I remembered faces,
expressions; I thought about the hospitality that I
had given my family and the home group that met
in our home. I pondered the hospitality that our
church dispensed in its various ministries and
support groups. Hospitality—that wonderful
quality of acceptance that begins in the heart and

welcomes people to pull up a chair to the table in our homes, our churches, or even our lives.

I picked up my pen and began to write as the happenings of the week started stacking up in my brain. Last week-end the kids had been home from college for Labor Day. Larry's mom and dad had driven over from Bakersfield on Sunday so we could celebrate Burl's birthday. Monday we had taken the kids and water-skied at Buena Vista Lake in Kern County. Tuesday began the usual work schedule and rituals of meshing with people at church. Our support ministries were open to anyone in the local community. As a church, we opened our arms to hurting and abused strugglers on the journey. There were Bible classes to teach, and for the past few days, I had filled in at the church office for a vacationing secretary.

As I sat now at this late-night hour, I wrote down the fleeting impressions that people had made on my heart. The awareness of the grace that God had given me was overwhelming. I was particularly sensitive to the weight of ministry and the hunger of people to be loved and noticed. These are the thoughts that flowed onto my paper:

ഉ

Sunday – a long day at our house,
    the pastor's house, and God's house.
It was wonderful.
I went to meet God –
    and He met me.
He filled my soul with a sense of His presence.

151

I worshiped and marveled again
　　that He loved me and had redeemed me.

I taught my Bible class.
We're studying holiness –
　　God's holiness and our pursuit of it.
We got off on the usual tangent:
　　the outside appearance,
　　and movies and drinking.
It reminded me of a scripture:
　　"Man looks on the outward appearance,
　　but God looks on the heart."
Lord, do we really love each other?
　　Or will we always get sidetracked
　　by the façade of appearances and actions?
Help me to grow in holiness
　　and grace, dear Lord.

My husband's folks were in church with us –
　　Visiting for the week-end.
So were our kids,
　　home from college for the holiday.
How good to sit together in a pew as a family.
I sneak peeks at Fern and Burl as their son
　　preaches.
　　　(Larry is still Fern's little boy).
There is pride mixed with a little bit of disbelief.
Is this man –
　　preaching with authority
　　and anointing
　　their son?

We ate dinner on the patio after church.
Balmy, desert weather – September weather –
  perfect weather.
I put steaks on the barbecue
  while Larry visited with his folks.

Annie and Scott talk to their Grandma,
  and tell me how big the house seems –
  compared to their dorm rooms.
After dinner, it's picture time.
I pose the family around Granddad –
  77 years old today.
Love hovers like an invisible halo around
  all of them.

Grandma and Granddad go home at four.
They leave our place in the Mojave desert
  where sand and skies go on forever,
  and huge cumulous clouds
  somersault in the canopy above us.
Lord, Thank you for helping me love the desert.
There were times I thought I'd hate it forever.
Now I breathe free in this spacious landscape.

I take a cake over to a friend's house.
She's giving a bridal shower tomorrow night for a
  gal at church.
We end up chatting by the car.
Dropping off a cake turned into a half-hour visit.
These people are special.
They help us pastor this church.

Their hearts are as big as our desert
    when it comes to people who hurt.
    Divorce recovery, substance abuse,
    home groups – they organize and
    listen and care.
So I took time to stop.
    "How are you two?
    We love you – appreciate you so much."
How often do I forget to take time
    just to visit with people?

Church was unusual tonight.
Were we all just tired?
    Or was it lethargy?
    Or passiveness?
I don't know.
    (I was tired too.)
No one seemed to respond to the worship time.
    (Had we not come to meet God again?)
Larry stopped everything
    and asked us to kneel.
We bowed our knees
    and our hearts.
Finally we started to worship.
We took Annie out for pie and coffee after church.
    (Scott had stayed home to study,
    so we had her all to ourselves).
She bubbled and chattered and
    hung on her dad's arm
    as we walked into the coffee shop.
(I love that she loves him so much.
    I love that she listens to him, respects him.)

Cindy came by our table to take our order.
  (She used to go to our church.
  Then her marriage floundered . . .
  and so did she.
  We saw less and less of her).

"Hi, Cindy. How're you doing?"
  we asked.
She stared into space above our heads,
  took a deep breath,
  then looked right into our eyes.
"Not good.
  I got divorced several months ago.
  Chuck doesn't help with expenses at all.
  He's got the car.
  I've been riding my bicycle to work."
She spoke in a one-breath, run-on monotone.

"Cindy," I interrupted her,
  "you live on the other side of town!
  It's not safe to ride your bike to work at night!"
She jabbed at tears that erupted.
  "I know. But it's all I've got."

She started unloading
  ("sharing" we say in church)
  and talked and talked.
Thank goodness it wasn't very busy.
We listened . . .
  with our ears and our eyes and our hearts.
"Come back anytime you want, Cindy.

We've got this divorce recovery group.
　　It's really supportive.
　　Maybe we can even help you with a car."
Cindy smiled – seemed relieved –
　　maybe glad we weren't judging her.

My heart ached.
Annie hadn't said a word –
　　just listened intently.
Lord, let her hear and learn:
　　Be very careful who you marry, Ann.

Monday morning. . .
　　we're going water-skiing with the kids!
Scott and Larry hook up the boat,
　　I pack a picnic lunch –
　　And off we go!
The day is tranquil with clear skies.
The water is smooth as glass, placid.
I sit on the shore,
　　book in my lap,
　　as the kids get ready to ski.
Larry turns the key;
　　the engine exhales in a throaty rumble.
　　Scott waits on the edge of the water,
　　ski resting on the surface.
"Ready!" he yells.
The boat roars into action.
Scott skims away from me,
　　straight, tall, swooshing back and forth
　　over the wakes.

I marvel again at the strong bodies of my
    children,
    agile, healthy, tanned . . .
    "Fearfully and wonderfully made,
    knit together in my womb."
God, they are such incredible miracles of your
    design

They've been skiing every summer for years.
Now they talk of the days when they'll marry,
    and bring their babies out here to ski
    just like we did with them.
Those will be great days, Lord,
    if you tarry.
Me – holding a grandbaby instead of a book!
    I smile to think about it.

Later that day, we're home again.
The kids pack up their books,
    folded laundry,
    and homemade cookies.
And off they go – back to school.

Standing on the curb, I wave good-by
    to the back of their car.
Then I shower, dress, and go to the bridal party.
The 38-year-old bride-to-be is ecstatic
    and full of wonder
    that she is actually, finally getting married . . .
    that all of these presents are for her –
    that all of these women are here to honor her.

She blushes and simpers over provocative
    nightgowns.
Lord, may they be very happy together –
    Mary and her Lawrence.

Tuesday I had errands to do.
I parked my car at my first destination.
A woman's voice was singing –
    not loudly but quite clearly.
I slowed my step to hear.
    ". . . happy birthday, dear Jimmy,
    happy birthday to you."
The voice came from a phone booth just down
    from the store.
Trying to appear nonchalant, I meandered
    toward her.
    A bag-lady stood in the booth,
    her cart stationed where she could see it.
She seemed to be caressing the phone she held to
    her mouth,
    cooing her words into the receiver.
A dirty, tattered, once-white straw hat was
    clamped over iron-gray hair,
    her turquoise sweat pants were smudged,
    hanging loosely on her spare frame.
    A baggy, yellow sweater engulfed the
    top half of her.
I heard her words as I passed the booth,
    standing in there –
    oblivious to anyone – everything else:
"Well now, my dear, you know,

these situations require a lot of
consideration . . . ."
The words were carefully enunciated,
the voice cultured, educated.
I was astonished,
and my heart broke.

Lord, how did she get to where she is now?
Pushing a cart around
with just a few paltry possessions –
"All her worldly goods."
Does she ever get to take a shower?
Wash her clothes?

Lord, who is she talking to?
Does anyone love her?
Do they know how she's living?

Robot-like, I finished my errands.
Where does she sleep at night, Lord?
When I got home,
I put groceries away,
straightened up the kids' rooms,
washed the sheets and towels,
folding them into neat squares,
and stacked them in the linen closet.

Lord, I wonder if the lady in the phone booth ever
lived in a house,
took care of a family,
cooked, cleaned, washed clothes,

and stacked things on shelves in her linen
closet?
Did she start out like the waitress?
Life all in order one day – married with children?
  Then – boom! Husband leaves,
  divorce happens,
  rides a bicycle,
  waits on tables just to make ends meet?
Lord, how many people like her are out there?

Wednesday, I spent the day with God.
I needed to be replenished on the inside.
I've been talking to too many people,
  going too many places.
This thing of what I am,
  who I am,
  what I do . . .
Is a role I have because of who my husband is.
The role is a privileged mantle,
  albeit a heavy one.

Help me, Lord,
  to always be sincere,
  to always have the right heart,
  and the right motives.

So this morning I sink into my wingback chair,
  the one in the corner by the blazing fireplace.
I feel drained, weary, depleted.

Turning to my daily reading in the Bible,
  I started reading the Prophet Isaiah

and couldn't stop.
All of the words are either shouting at me
or whispering into the inner recesses of my soul.
Finally I started to pray.
I talked to God,
and He talked to me,
and I wept before the wonder and the majesty
of who He is and what He is to me.

Lord, you love me (I'm so grateful . . .),
and you love the waitress,
and the bag lady.
Will you speak to them, too, please?
Will you help them?

That night I got my house ready for our home
group.
They come every Wednesday.
I want them to feel peace and acceptance when
they walk in the door.
So I vacuum, dust, light candles,
and make coffee and set out cups.
God, bless everyone who meets here tonight.

After greeting the home group leaders,
I hurry to the church a few blocks away to
meet Larry.
One of the ushers stops me as I walk into the
foyer.
"Jean, could you talk to this young man for a
minute?"
A nice-looking Hispanic man holds out his hand

as we're introduced.
He starts a litany as soon as Norm leaves.
His wife left two weeks ago.
She wants a divorce.
He's devastated and wants her back.
 She's just had her seventh miscarriage;
 she was abused as a child,
 raped as a young girl;
 never felt loved by her parents.
His counselor sent him to our church –
 to our Divorce Recovery Group.
I take both of his hands in mine.
"Do you believe in God
 and that He cares about you?"
"Yes, yes," he answers vehemently.
"Good! We're going to pray for you and your wife.
 She's hurting very badly,
 and she's probably angry about losing all
 those babies.
 Let's pray."
We pray, he smiles, and I walk with him to Divorce
 Recovery.

Oh, dear God, can you –
 will you glue this one back together?
 Will they trust You to do it?

Later, at home, Rosie is cleaning up my kitchen.
I chat with her.
 "How are you doing since your miscarriage?"
She stops what she's doing,
 her eyes film over with unshed tears.

"I'm doing better.
I appreciate all the prayers so much.
It's nothing, though, like what you must have
    felt when your five-year-old died."
I listen to her – the two of us mothers talking.
    The enormity of my former pain doesn't
    diminish the very real pain she's feeling.
I tell her that,
    and give her a hug.
Rosie pats my back with soapy hands,
    and hangs on tightly for just a moment.

Thursday morning –
Time for Ladies' Intercessory Prayer Hour.
These women love you Lord.
Many of them are needy,
    but they know you
    and are trying
    to trust you even more with their
    impossibilities.
Give us all increased faith
    in who You are and
    in what you (alone, Lord!) can do.

Later, after teaching my Bible Study class,
    I took one of our women's leaders out to lunch.
Mommy of one and pregnant with another,
    I sat across from her at lunch
    and we talked.
I didn't have an agenda;
    This wasn't a "meeting."
I just wanted to show her the face of a friend,

someone who appreciated all her work with
    our women.
This very dignified, self-possessed lady opened up
    to me.
Yesterday she had spent the whole morning
    in the Welfare Department
    applying for assistance.

Her husband lost his job,
    they guard every penny,
    but there's no insurance for this baby
    that's coming.
Sarah is diminished today.
She's been sorely dehumanized by an institution.
It's taken a toll and she's quiet
    and doesn't laugh quite so readily.
And yet, Lord, she does still smile.
    Help them, Lord.
Thank God you're not an institution.
    When we take one step toward you,
    You run toward us.
    Run toward Sarah and Matt, God.

That evening I ran a piping hot bubble bath in
    the bathtub,
    lit a rosy pink candle,
    and filled a crystal, stemmed goblet with iced
    water.
Dipping slowly into the frothy concoction,
    I took my latest escape book,
    James Herriott's, *Every Living Thing,*
    and started reading and melting.

164

Chuckling occasionally, I read the anecdotes
about animals in need of a doctor.
And then, a warm, caring veterinarian comes
along and provides just the right touch
that makes everything better.
That's what you do, Lord.
You come along and provide just the right touch;
You make everything better.

The next morning –
Larry and I prayed together in the sanctuary
before we went into the office
to start our work day.
The strength of our joined hands and hearts
cements me closer, if possible, to him . . .
and to you, God.

We both worked hard all day.
Larry's only study day turned into a
"being-with-people" kind of day.
Lord, give him extra grace and strength
as he ends up studying all day tomorrow . . .
like he usually does.

Give me grace, too, dear Lord.
I wish we could spend Saturdays together –
like we used to –
before he was the senior pastor.
Sometimes I'm ambivalent about his role of
shepherd.
You've called him to be one,
but the sheep take up so much of his time!

Could you send a Jethro to give him some advice?

The voices of staff pastors and secretaries
    rise around me as I wash coffee cups
    at the end of the day.
Laughing, animated, they're making plans for
    tonight,
    plans for tomorrow. . .
    videos, picnics, Magic Mountain,
They've worked hard all week;
    they're wonderful pastors, too.
Bless them, God.

Larry and I go home.
Another week has evaporated.
Where does the time go, Lord?
Does it all just become part of our personal
    histories?
People and memories stored in treasuries of our
    hearts?
Give me the heart of a shepherdess
    as I walk alongside my husband.
Cause us both to keep becoming more like you,
    Jesus.
Thank you for grace and strength and wonder
    throughout this week.

(Written in Lancaster, California, October 2, 1992).

Husband, children, parents, friends, and bag
ladies—the week had been full! I sipped a cup of
chamomile tea in the comfort of my home as strong

166

winds whipped through our cedar trees outside. Suddenly I understood how strong God's grace had been to me that week. I was immensely aware of the privilege of touching the lives of people.

I whispered a prayer for Larry, for Scott and Annie, and for Cindy and the bag lady. Thank you, God, for your strength. Help me to offer my-*self* and my home in the spirit of hospitality that flows out of a heart full of you. Keep my heart attentive to all of your children . . . everywhere.

ℒ *Reflect* ~ Do I "see" people as I travel my journey? Do I truly "hear" what they are saying? Am I aware of the misfortune of others? Do I attempt to live in my own strength? Does the essence of hospitality flow out of my living?

ℒ *Respond* ~ I will ask God to make me sensitive to other people; to hear them and see them the way God does. I will do what I can to encourage every individual I encounter—even if it is only a smile. And I will pray for the dear ones who need the touch of God on their hearts. I will ask God for His grace and strength to make me strong. I will open the door of my home and offer a cup of coffee—or tea—in the name of Jesus.

ℒ

"'My grace is sufficient for you, for power is perfected in weakness.' Most gladly, therefore, I will

rather boast about my weaknesses, that the power of Christ may dwell in me. Therefore I am well content with weaknesses, with insults, with distresses, with persecutions, with difficulties, for Christ's sake; for when I am weak, then I am strong." (2 Corinthians 12:9-10 NAS)

℘

He giveth more grace as our burdens grow
   greater.
He sendeth more strength as our labors
   increase;
To added afflictions He addeth His mercy,
To multiplied trials He multiplies peace.

When we have exhausted our store of
   endurance,
When our strength has failed ere the day is half
   done,
When we reach the end of our hoarded resources
Our Father's full giving is only begun.

His love has no limits, His grace has no
   measure.
His power no boundary known unto men;
For out of His infinite riches in Jesus
He giveth, and giveth, and giveth again.

(Annie J. Flint—Public Domain)

❦ Chapter Fourteen ❧

Come to the Table

*"Relationships are meant to be signs of God's
love for humanity as a whole and
each person in particular."*
(Henri J. M. Nouwen)

I watched the clock in the stifling classroom and willed the hands to move faster. Grocery shopping, menus, and school assignments occupied my mind. The professor went from student to student asking them to share the topic of their final research paper with the class. I had answered, "Zora Neale Hurston," when he came to me, and then promptly resumed my mental tasks. I was jolted away from my anxious thoughts by a soft voice that said with quiet intensity, "I am going to write a paper on how much Americans hate anybody from the Arabian and Persian world."

The young woman instantly had everyone's attention. Her pretty olive-skinned, oval face was framed by the typical chador worn by a modest Muslim woman. I had been vaguely aware of her during the semester, but now my curiosity was fully engaged.

There are over eighty ethnic and cultural groups of people in South Orange County in this area of Southern California. When I began my re-entry into the educational world at a community college close to my home, I noticed the occasional women on campus who wore chadors, burqas, saris, and African robes and headgear. This particular young woman who spoke out so bravely that day in our English class was a refugee from Afghanistan.

The Oklahoma City bombing had taken place a year before. When Khatal announced her paper topic that day to the class, she gave the reasons for her choice. She and her family had suffered great bias because of their ethnicity.

"Our people got blamed for the bombing before anyone even knew who did it," she explained. "My husband and I received threats and hate calls on the telephone. And why? Because of our last name." They lived in San Francisco at the time of the tragedy. As the whole country reacted in horror to the bombing, Khatal and her family were targeted with persecution and accusations that deeply scarred this young immigrant wife and mother.

My heart ached as I listened to her explanation. How could I persuade her that most Americans were not hateful people? I scribbled a short note to her apologizing for the actions of a very few people. On the note, I gave her my phone number and address and wrote that I would love to have her come to my house sometime for tea. As I left the classroom that day, I smiled as I tucked the note in her hand and rushed to my next class.

That night she called me on the phone. She said she would love to come to my house. Full of curiosity and skepticism, her husband had asked her, "What kind of woman is this?"

Her heavily accented voice continued, "I told him you are very kind in everything you say in class; that you are very wise in what you say."

Just a few days later, Khatal came to my house. Her large brown eyes were soft and luminous and hinted of a desire for friendship. Almost shyly, she handed me the bouquet of fresh flowers which were cradled in her arms. Her formal but gracious mannerisms and way of speaking resonated with an old-world charm. Khatal was beautiful!—so different from my white skin, blue eyes, and blond hair.

Now I was shy. Would I be able to convince this immigrant woman of my sincere wish to show the face of an American friend by offering my hospitality? Khatal immediately put me at ease with her innate cultural courtesies. Looking around my home with unabashed curiosity, she exclaimed how beautiful it was. I thanked her as I led her to the dining room, pointing out the pictures of my children hanging on the wall. Our little dog, Max, sniffed at her long skirt as she swirled through my living room admiring my children and my paintings. While I put her flowers in a vase, she chattered gracefully about her continued amazement that I had invited her to my house.

She was making conversation so easy! We visited comfortably as I prepared my refreshments.

I served dream bars and shortbread cookies. Pouring tea from my Grandmother Olson's antique burgundy teapot, I explained a little background of my Norwegian heritage—that my grandparents were emigrants to this country, and I was a second-generation American. We sat at my table and drank tea as the afternoon wore on.

Deeply religious, Khatal shared some of the principles of her Muslim faith. It was her culture, her religion, and her heritage. I shared my love for God and my deep faith. I gave her some glimpses into my life as a pastor's daughter and the concepts of holiness that my dad and mom instilled in me. As we talked and sipped tea from my loveliest teacups, we began building a bridge to each other across cultures and across misunderstandings.

Khatal described the painful and difficult experience of leaving Afghanistan with her family. I gained a clearer picture of what it was like to be a refugee. They were without a home and a country for several years until they finally found a distant relative in the United States who could sponsor them. They ricocheted between the countries of Italy and England until they were finally allowed to legally come to America. She was only fourteen when her family left the terror of a Russian-occupied homeland.

With disarming candor, Khatal enlightened me about some cultural practices of her people. Smiling, with eyes sparkling, she told me about the marriage her father had arranged for her when she was just a teenager. She never saw her husband before their wedding day. It was several nights before the marriage was consummated. In the conspiratorial tone that women use with each other when they are speaking of intimate things, Khatal told me candidly that she would not sleep with her husband at first. With lowered voice, she leaned toward me and confided private details of her first nights with her husband. They are too private to share with you, dear reader, but my heart melded with Khatal's as she described her husband and her marriage.

"Now I love my husband very much. We have beautiful children . . . and I am pregnant now with twins!"

I listened and marveled at the fascinating customs and rituals of another culture. Drinking tea with Khatal was a custom that forced us to relax and listen to each other with our hearts. We had so much in common! Women who are wives and mothers and who have a strong faith share a kindred spirit. No outer garment can cover up our hearts. Khatal hugged me that day before she left my home. She had seen the heart of a woman who had welcomed her to the hearth of her home. Hopefully, my friendship began to chip away at the stereotype of a vengeful American.

Soon after our introductory tea, Khatal invited me to visit her mother and father's apartment in Irvine. When I crossed their threshold, I stepped into another country. The rugs, the furnishings, the wall hangings were of another world. The mother and Khatal's sisters had huge welcoming smiles. They gave slight bows and motioned me to a seat on the couch. Delectable aromas wafted through the tiny apartment. The women served delicate little pastries they had made. The mother beamed and nodded her head vigorously as we sipped tea and attempted to understand each other. Khatal was the only one who spoke English, and so she served as an interpreter. Her children and an assortment of nieces and nephews lined the walls with fingers in their mouths as they stared at me with wide eyes. I held Khatal's toddler in my lap and sipped the tea and tasted the foods of Afghanistan.

Several months later, I was invited to a baby shower for Khatal. Just before the birth of her babies, she called me with a desperate request. There was a heart defect in one of her babies. The doctors were determining whether or not they should perform surgery on her little boy while he was still in the womb. I was one of the first people she called. "Please pray for my baby that he will be all right," she pleaded. My heart contracted with concern. I assured Khatal of my love and my prayers.

Khatal and her family moved out of the area a year or so after the birth of her twins. For a few years we exchanged notes and Christmas cards, and then I lost track of them. I thought often, though, of how wonderful it was that the finger of God had nudged the two of us together from such diverse backgrounds. We had reached out to each other across a great divide. Something as refined and gracious and hospitable as a cup of tea had helped to bridge the great gulf that had loomed between us.

There is nothing like asking someone to "come to the table" in striving to break down barriers. I pray that in this nation, in this world, many more of us will brew some pots of tea and extend an invitation to those who need to hear those magical, melding words of "welcome to the table." I firmly believe God's desire is for all of us around the globe to experience that mysterious blending that makes community.

For a brief moment in time, Khatal and I stood together, strong in our common bond of friendship; strong in the passions that stir the hearts of women in every culture. I learned that one little act of kindness, the sacred ritual of sharing tea in my home, was able to transcend and overcome the inherent misunderstandings that so often divide people of different cultures. My dining room table was the laboratory that distilled our differences to the human level of affection and friendship.

№ *Reflect* ~ Do I shy away from people of other cultures? Am I willing to open the doors of my life to other cultures and ethnicities?

№ *Respond* ~ I will be open to opportunities to

176

meet people who are different than me. I will experience the rich tapestry of other lives and cultures as I welcome people to come to the table of my life and home.

"Love your neighbor as yourself. Love does no wrong to anyone, so love satisfies all of God's requirements." (Romans 13:10 NLT)

ဢ

Some seem to be born with a nearly
*   completed puzzle.*
And so it goes.
Souls going this way and that
Trying to assemble the myriad parts.

But know this. No one has within
*   themselves*
All the pieces to their puzzle.
Like before the days when they used to
*   seal*
jigsaw puzzles in cellophane. Insuring
*   that*
all the pieces were there.

Everyone carries with them at least one
*   and probably*
Many pieces to someone else's puzzle.
Sometimes they know it.
Sometimes they don't.

177

And when you present your piece
Which is worthless to you,
To another, whether you know it or not,
Whether they know it or not,
You are a messenger from the Most High.[8]

Lawrence Kushner

---

[8] Kushner, Lawrence. From *Honey from the Rock.* *Spiritual Literacy: Reading the Sacred in Everyday Life.* New York: Scribner. 1996. 422.

⤜ Chapter Fifteen ⤛

Home is Where the Hearth Is

*"The cornerstone in Truth is laid, / The guardian walls
of Honor made, / The roof of Faith is built above, /
The fire upon the hearth is Love, / Though rains
descend and loud winds call, / This happy
home shall never fail."*
(John Oxenham)

My home is my sanctuary. It comforts me
and gives me warmth from the cold and pressures
of the outside world. I live and move and have my
being in my home. It is an extension of who I am
because it reflects what I like. Books are stacked
on shelves and tables in every room of the house. I
love painted walls and flowers and cozy corners.
My poor husband once requested, "Pick out any
wallpaper you want . . . just please no more
flowers!" when I announced I was going to redo a
bedroom. The bottom line is that the two of us
have created a home from the house we bought so
many years ago. Our home—this sanctuary—is
warmed with the love we have for each other and
with the love of God which dwells within our
hearts. The hearth of our home is not the fireplace;

it is the presence of a living God who warms us with His love.

The walls of the houses in which we've lived over the years have soaked up the stories of our family. They have been silent witnesses to joy and happiness, heartache, anger, tears, belly laughs, and long quiet periods of contentment when all is well with our world. We have wound the grandfather clock that stands in our entryway countless times over the years as the seasons of our lives have ticked away. Mark Twain once described his home in this manner: *"To us, our house [. . .] had a heart and soul and eyes to see us with and approvals and solicitudes and deep sympathies. It was of us, and we were in its confidence and lived in its grace and in the peace of its benediction. [. . .] To me it was a holy place and beautiful."*[9]

My home is a holy place to me, also. It's the backdrop as I put the teakettle on and welcome people into my home and into my life.

Traditions and Rituals

Traditions and rituals are the elements of stability in a constantly changing world. They are acted out in sacred ceremonies that connect us to the moment and to our loved ones. *"Our homes can become sacred places, filled with life and meaning. We do not need cathedrals to remind ourselves to*

---

[9] Twain, Mark. *Essays and Sketches of MARK TWAIN.* New York: Barnes & Noble Books. 1995. 472.

experience the sacred."[10]   The sacred ceremonies can be simple or elaborate, but they should be meaningful. They can be holiday celebrations, meals around a table, games played in front of a blazing fireplace, birthday cakes, and quiet times of reading and reflection or watching a favorite movie together. A life and home without sacred ritual are devoid of meaning. Ordinary, everyday activities become sacred when we pray over them and infuse them with care and attention.

People today have houses with many rooms—living rooms where no one lives, kitchens where no one cooks, dining rooms where no one eats together, and bedrooms filled with the noise of a television set. Our big houses give us shelter, but they don't necessarily offer us sanctuary.

Too often our families are disconnected individuals locked away from each other in their own rooms. Dr. Dobson does much to motivate families to become strong in their relationships. He writes: *"The great value of traditions come as they give a family a sense of identity, a 'belongingness.' All of us desperately need to feel that we're not just a cluster of people living together in a house, but we're a family that's conscious of its uniqueness, its personality, character and heritage, and that our special relationships of love and companionship make us a unit with identity and personality."* Ask yourself what traditions and rituals cement your children into the structure of your home, your

---

[10] Norris, Gunilla. *Spiritual Literacy: Reading the Sacred in Everyday Life.* New York: Scriber. 1996. 80.

family. Frenetic activities, fast-food, speeding from one event to the next are divisive to the unity of a family. There is nothing sacred in rushing around, constantly tuned in to the noise of the world.

Be aware of sacred opportunities to savor the wonder of the outdoors with your child, to examine the color of the sky; to listen to birds chirping overhead. Sit around a table with family and friends and enact rituals of discussion and exploration of the mind. Those are the moments that your child will remember—the scared rituals and traditions of everyday living that become extraordinary occasions embedded in his and her memory.

Experts have noted that family rituals and bonding together as a unit are especially important for children. *"Belonging and feeling respected and heard—that's something we can give somebody at home. Most other places—school, work, social events—we are being evaluated. The dining table is the ideal location to remedy this modern-day dilemma and to create traditions and memories that last a lifetime."*[11] Gourmet cooking and elaborate menus are not important considerations when you prepare meals for your family and friends. The most sumptuous table, the most luxurious house cannot compensate for an emptiness of the soul—a home that does not offer comfort and acceptance.

Keep your heart attentive and the food you serve wholesome. *"A bowl of soup with someone*

---

[11] Margaret Mackenzie, Ph.D., nutritional anthropologist. Article from Orange County Register.

you love is better than steak with someone you hate" (Proverbs 17:13 NLT). It is the love and listening and conversation you cultivate that will make your house a home.

Soul Food

Soul food doesn't necessarily have to be about culture; it has to do with making memories and feeding the body and the soul. Many of our traditions and rituals are wrapped around food. Food becomes sacramental in this thing of creating the sacred in our lives. We do far more than feed people when they come to the table and share a meal in our homes. They feel the welcome of our hearts as we invite them to the table. We feed their souls as we listen to them, serve them, and ask if they want seconds. Breaking bread together evokes commonality and community. When people are seated around a table, side by side, they are on common ground, on the same level.

Remember the round little Pillsbury doughboy in commercials from long ago? His wrap-up statement—arms spread wide with a cheery smile on his chubby face—was, "Nothing says lovin' like somethin' from the oven!" Let others sniff the aroma of food wafting through the house as they walk in your back door. Whether it is home-made or emptied onto plates from cartons, it will smell wonderful and say, "Welcome home," to your family.

Food is a powerful identity marker. A

supper was the last ritual Jesus had with his followers before He departed to the place where He knew He would be arrested and later crucified. Eating with their master marked those men as being His disciples. They were the only people Jesus had invited to this last meal. He had taught them repeatedly that "people need more than bread for their life; real life comes by feeding on every word of the LORD" (Deuteronomy 8:3).

So often we feed our body, but we starve our souls. We are body, mind, and spirit—tripartite beings made in the image of God. When we feed our body with nourishing food that gives us strength and energy, we would do well to remember to feed the soul as well. Just as we cannot live without food, we must feed our souls with the richness of God's Word and nurture our spirits during times of prayer. Remember, we serve the needs of people emotionally and relationally from a full heart, not a starved spirit.

Going to the Kitchen

The kitchen is alchemical,
A place where we cook—actually
And spiritually. We come to it
for nourishment and ease.
We come to it as to a center—

The heart of the house,
The heart of dwelling.

In the kitchen we are one,
Linked by hunger—
actual hunger and spiritual hunger.

We go to the kitchen to be
Nourished and revealed.
It is a holy place.[12]

—*Gunilla Norris*

Let the holy place of the kitchen be the center of your home where you prepare food for the body; let Christ be the center of your life as you feast on the food He has for your soul.

The Hearth of the Home

What do I mean by that phrase, "Home is where the *hearth* is?" I did some research that fascinated me. We are encouraged throughout the New Testament to edify each other. *Edify* means to uplift, enlighten, or encourage, particularly in moral or religious knowledge, or in faith and holiness. The word *edify* is derived from the Latin word *aedes* which means "house or temple," and it is coupled with the word *facio*—"to make." Thus we conclude that *edify,* in an archaic sense, means to make; to build a house or a temple.

---

[12] Norris, Gunilla. "Becoming Bread." *Spiritual Literacy: Reading the Sacred in Everyday Life.* New York: Scribner. 1996. 522.

In Roman mythology, Vesta was the goddess of the home, the guardian of their familial temple. The hearth was the center of family life in ancient Rome. Vesta's symbol was the fire in the hearth. In that ancient culture, it was the custom for families to gather around a common fire—often located in an atrium—a hearth where the food was cooked, and the family was warmed as they talked about the events of the day. It was important not to let the fire go out; someone had to tend it daily to make sure the embers were always burning. If the fire went out, they had to borrow fire from a neighboring home and carry it back to their hearth.

The apostle Paul was a Roman citizen, familiar with the mythological beliefs of the culture. It is very likely that he often passed by Vesta's temple in the Forum and witnessed the duties performed by the Vestal Virgins as they tended her sacred flame.

As Paul tramped around the city and wrote his letters to new converts, he used the metaphor of the human body as a temple. Perhaps he even had that analogy in mind when he penned these words in his epistle to the church at Corinth: *"Don't you know that your body is the temple of the Holy Spirit, who lives in you and was given to you by God? You do not belong to yourself, for God bought you with a high price. So you must honor God with your body"* (1 Corinthians 6:19—20 NLT).

In another scripture, we read that the Holy Spirit appeared *"like flames or tongues of fire [. . .] and settled on each of them. And everyone present was filled with the Holy Spirit [. . .] "* (Acts 2:3—4 NLT). Fire—a flame—is, therefore, a symbol of the Holy Spirit that the universal Church recognizes. John, another apostle, writes in his first epistle that we "have an anointing from the Holy One" (1 John 2:20 NAS). The anointing came from the indwelling presence of the Holy Spirit in the body of a believer; it also was a ritual performed to anoint someone as a priest or king. Oil was poured over the head during the anointing ceremony. Oil was also used as the fuel that burned in lamps to provide light in households in ancient days.

In 1 Peter 2:5 we read these incredible words: *"And now God is building you, as living stones, into his spiritual temple. What's more, you are God's holy priests, who offer the spiritual sacrifices that please Him because of Jesus Christ"* (NLT). If we connect these scriptures and keep in mind who we are as Christians and followers of Jesus Christ, we build a powerful image: I am—my body is—the temple of the Holy Spirit whose symbol is a flame of fire. But it is God who is *making* me, *building* me into His spiritual temple, and I am His holy priest. With that indwelling presence and anointing of the Holy Spirit, I fan the flame that blazes within my soul by my passion for Jesus Christ and my love and communion with Him.

Home is where the hearth is . . . my heart, Christ's home, is warmed by the presence of the Holy Spirit. My body is the sanctuary of God's indwelling Spirit, and my home is the sanctuary in which I live by the grace and blessing of God.

Hospitality

When people come to my house, when they sit around my table, they partake of *me*—the essence that flows from within. And yet, my-*self* is crucified with Christ, and it is Christ who lives in me (Galatians 2:20). It is the presence of Jesus that people are attracted to in me—if I am practicing His presence and filled with His Holy Spirit.

This book has been about giving of one's self by being *attentive* to the moment and by being *intentional* in serving others. My home is a holy place where I long for family and friends to be edified when they pull up a chair and push close to the table. I was raised by a mother and father who welcomed every friend and many strangers to our table. They served many cups of coffee and gave a blessing "in the name of Jesus." I am as liable to give a cup of coffee as I am to serve a pot of tea, but whatever it is that my hand does, I pray it will encourage the one I serve. I pray that I bless and glorify my Heavenly Father by giving cups of tea and a listening heart in the name of Jesus.

Home is where the hearth is. Fan the flame that is in you (2 Timothy 1:6) and welcome people to your presence. They will feel the touch of Jesus as you love them. We do what we do because we are who we are. You are the temple of the Holy

Spirit—go and share the warmth with those who are cold and lonely.

As you read this book, I offered you a glimpse into my heart. My body is the temple of the Spirit of God. And so, as you read, I have symbolically invited you to come to the table of who I am and partake of me. I pray that you have nibbled on some nutritious fare; I pray that it creates a hunger in you to let your life become a feast that others partake of.

In making a pot of tea, I have made a ceremony of serving others. And as our Novel Tea group has met every month, we have created rituals that nourish us and steady us in unsteady times. These rituals remind us that we are thinking people; we are people whose souls are touched by words; we are people who break bread together. Every ritual cements us into the sacraments of yesterday, and hints of the rites we hope to continue performing tomorrow.

Ask God to be creative in you and through you. Perhaps you feel the need for deeper relationships in your life. Create some rituals, dare to let others peek into your soul as you offer yourself in friendship. You will find yourself looking forward to tomorrow. God bless you as begin striding forward on that road of excellence in your daily living.

໖ଠ

Laid on Thine altar, O my Lord divine,
Accept this gift today for Jesus' sake;
I have no jewels to adorn Thy shrine,
No far-famed sacrifice to make;
But here within my trembling hand I bring
This will of mine, a thing that seemeth small.
But Thou alone, O Lord, canst understand
How when I yield Thee this,
I yield mine all.

Recipes
for
Delicious Fare

To enjoy at your
Teas and Luncheons

Buttermilk Raisin Scones

3 cups flour
1/3 cup sugar

2 ½ tsp. baking powder
½ tsp. baking soda

¾ tsp. salt
¾ cup butter,
  softened
½ cup raisins
1 cup buttermilk

There are few things more satisfying to teatime-lovers
than scones fresh from the oven. Preheat oven to 400
degrees. In large bowl, combine flour, sugar, baking
powder, baking soda, and salt. Add butter or margarine
and beat with electric mixer until well blended. Add
raisins, then pour in buttermilk and mix until blended.
Shape dough into a ball and divide in half. Roll
into two circles, about ¾ inch think, on a lightly floured
surface. Cut each circle into eight wedges. Bake on
lightly greased baking sheet for 12—15 minutes, or
until golden. Serve warm with butter. Makes 16
delicious scones.

White Chocolate Scones

2 cups flour
2 ½ teaspoons baking powder
½ teaspoon salt
¼ to ½ cup sugar – to taste

6 tablespoons butter
(do not substitute)
½ to ¾ cups craisins
½ to ¾ cups white
chocolate chips

1 egg, slightly beaten, combined with enough buttermilk to make 1 cup

Combine flour, baking powder, salt, and sugar. Cut butter into this mixture with pastry cutter until it resembles coarse crumbs. Stir in egg with buttermilk until mixture holds together. Drop by teaspoonfuls onto an ungreased cookie sheet.
Bake in preheated 400-degree oven for 12—15 minutes.
Makes 12 generous or 24 smaller scones.

Whipped cream accompaniment:

1 pint whipping cream—whip until creamy

Mix together:
3 oz. cream cheese
1 teaspoon vanilla extract
1 teaspoon almond extract
1/2 cup powdered sugar

Gently fold into the whipped cream and serve with scones and jam, jelly, or curd.

Crème Vanilla*

1/2 cup sour cream
1 cup whipping cream

1 tablespoon sugar
1 teaspoon vanilla

In a glass jar, mix the creams together until well blended. Leave uncovered at room temperature for about 5 or 6 hours or until the crème has thickened.

Stir in sugar and vanilla. Cover and refrigerate. This crème will keep, refrigerated, for a week to ten days. Makes 1 ½ cups crème.

*This recipe for crème vanilla is very similar to the clotted cream that is served with scones in many teahouses. It is delicious and can also be spooned over puddings, fruits, or pies.

Cranberry-Peach Freezer Jam

3   cups fresh cranberries
2 cups chopped peaches
6 cups sugar
¾ cup peach nectar

1 tsp. ginger
2 pouches (3 oz. each)
  liquid pectin
¼ cup lemon juice

1. Process cranberries in processor until pieces are approximately 1/8 inch in size. Transfer to large bowl. Next process peaches until 1/4 inch in size. Add peaches, sugar, peach nectar and ginger to cranberries; stir 2 minutes. Let stand 10 minutes.

2. Combine pectin and lemon juice n small bowl; stir into fruit mixture. Stir 2 minutes to mix thoroughly.

3. Spoon into seven 1-cup freezer containers, leaving ½ inch space at top. Cover with tight-fitting lids. Let

stand 24 hours to set. Refrigerate up to three weeks or freeze up to six months.
(Makes seven 1-cup containers of jam.)

Bark Candy

This doesn't have peppermint, but is very fun—especially for kids!—when you use M&M candies. Prep Time: approx. 5 Minutes. Cook Time: approx. 3 minutes. Ready in approx. 15 Minutes. Makes 1 pound (16 servings).

1 (10 ounce) package vanilla baking chips
2 teaspoons vegetable oil
1 1/2 cups mini—candy coated chocolate pieces

Directions: Line a baking pan with wax paper or foil. In a microwave safe bowl combine vanilla chips and vegetable oil; microwave on high until chips are melted. Stir until smooth; let cool for 2 minutes. Stir in candy-coated chocolate pieces. Spread mixture onto prepared pan; chill for 10 minutes and break into pieces.

Note: Here are some delectable variations for your bark—coarsely chop salted macadamia nuts or cashews (the amount you desire) and add to the melted white chocolate before you spread it out to cool. Or you can use crushed peppermint candy, lemon drops or whatever suits your fancy. Yummy!

Fruity Bonbons

1/3 cup sugar

1/4 cup butter, softened

1/4 cup plus 2 tablespoons frozen orange juice
   concentrate, thawed and undiluted

1/4 cup honey

1 1/2 teaspoons grated orange rind

1 teaspoon vanilla extract

1 egg

1/2 cup plus 2 tablespoons all purpose flour

3/4 teaspoon ground cinnamon

1/8 teaspoon baking soda

1/8 teaspoon ground cloves

1/8 teaspoon ground allspice

1/2 cup dried cranberries

1/3 cup golden raisins

1/3 cup finely chopped dried apricots

3 tablespoons chopped almonds

Cream sugar and butter using an electric mixer set at medium speed until mixture is light and fluffy (about 5 minutes). Add juice concentrate, honey, orange rind, vanilla, and egg; beat at medium speed until blended. Combine flour, cinnamon, baking soda, cloves and allspice. With mixer running at low speed, gradually add to orange mixture. Stir in cranberries, raisins, apricots, and almonds. Spoon batter evenly into 33 paper lined miniature muffin pans. Bake at 350°F for 20 minutes or until lightly browned. Cool in pans 3 minutes; remove from pans and cool on wire rack.

Cheesecake-Topped Brownies Recipe

1 (21 1/2 oz) package brownie mix
1 (8 oz) package cream cheese; softened
2 tablespoons butter or margarine, softened
1 tablespoon cornstarch
1 (14 oz) can sweetened condensed milk
1 egg
1 teaspoon vanilla extract
1 (16 oz) container prepared chocolate frosting

Preheat oven to 350°F. Grease a 9 by 13 inch baking pan. Prepare brownie mix according to the directions on the package. Spread into prepared baking pan. In a medium bowl, beat cream cheese, butter and cornstarch until fluffy. Gradually beat in sweetened condensed milk, egg and vanilla until smooth. Pour cream cheese mixture evenly over brownie batter. Bake for 45 minutes, or until top is lightly browned. Allow to cool, spread with frosting and cut into bars. (Or drizzle with a thick chocolate sauce)

Jean's Hawaiian Chicken Salad

2 – cans Tyson chicken breast (premium chunk) – drain off liquid
1 – 20 oz. can pineapple tidbits – drained (reserve the juice in a cup)
1 large Washington delicious apples, cored, diced in chunks (do not peel – red peel adds color and fiber)

198

2 stalks celery – thinly sliced on a slant
1/2 to 3/4 cups chopped walnuts
1 cup loosely packed coconut

Gently mix together in bowl, and then add dressing.

Dressing:

1 cup mayonnaise (may use low-fat)
1/2 to 1 tsp. curry   (use to taste – I prefer the milder flavor)
dash of salt and white pepper

Add approximately 1/4 cup of reserved pineapple juice to mixture. Using a whip, mix until blended and it has a creamy consistency. Add more juice until mayonnaise is sufficiently thinned. Be careful! Do not get the dressing too runny! Go by taste (will be sweeter as you add more juice) and consistency.

Pour dressing over salad ingredients and mix gently but thoroughly. Store in refrigerator for several hours or overnight to let flavors blend. Serve in a pretty bowl if for a buffet, or on beds of shredded lettuce placed on pretty individual plates. Serves app. 7—8.

What Readers are saying about A Novel Tea:

- "I desperately needed encouragement. It inspired me to have people for tea that need support, and *maybe* I will start my own book club!" Sharri, Wheaton, Illinois.

- "I just finished *A Novel Tea*! I am ready to join your book club. What a wonderful story, great friends, and memorable experiences. I think your book should be in every church library!" Peggy, Evergreen, Colorado.

- "I would love to start a book club [like A Novel Tea] when I get back to Chile." Dodey, Chile, South America.

- "I read your book so often, especially when I need some encouragement. The book is well-written and very inspirational." Pat Wright in Virginia.

- "Your book is just delightful and very motivational to do contagious Christianity. I am taking the book to a dear friend in the morning to see if she would like to join me in starting [A Novel Tea].   What I liked is that you give several variations that would accomplish the same purpose. I liked that you included the list of books and recipes and many ideas on how to carry out the plan." Dawn Anna in Phoenix, Arizona.

- "Your stories, instructions, and poems touched my soul. I must tell you that one word really jumped out at me—you used the word 'hibernate.' I think that describes what I have been doing these past few years in making excuses for not being as hospitable as I should be. Thank you for the encouragement your words have been to me. As I read your book, God dropped a gentle thought into my brain: Why not meet with the mothers of the children in my class for lunch on a weekly or monthly basis? It would not be a fancy tea, but what an opportunity to build a rapport with parents." Karen, a kindergarten teacher in Lancaster, California.

- "Thank you for such a masterpiece of glimpses into your own wonderful heart and really into the heart and cry of humanity." Betty in Riverside, California.

- "What a wonderful, refreshing book—it really challenged me to have more special times with those I love and to reach out more to others." Sharon in Coeur d'Alene, Idaho.

- "My favorite chapter was 'Tea by the Sea . . . Just Annie and Me.' I was glad to the see the pictures of you and Annie. It spurs me on to want to make more intentional special times with my daughter, Jill." Julie in Grover Beach, California.

- "What a beautiful book. I'm chair of the Women's Ministry and Altar Guild at St. John's Lutheran Church and I see ways to utilize your 'Novel Tea' ideas throughout Women's Ministry!" Donna in Bakersfield, California.

- "I loved your book! You have truly inspired me! My mother is visiting me from Florida. I'm planning a special tea for her and my college-age daughter. I also went back to school to finish my degree at age 43. I'm going to read some of your classics over the summer." Sandy in Selma, California.

- "I can't thank you enough for Jean's book. I read the chapter about the Angel of Hope and shed a tear or two. She has such a way with words." from Joan in Bakersfield, California who sent *A Novel Tea* to Shirley, a mother whose adult son was killed in a trucking accident.

The author would love to hear your comments about her book. Please contact her at:

www.springbrookpress.com or write:
Jean Chapman, P. O. Box 423, East Irvine,
California 92650-0423.